D1474108

Lean Down Your Ear
upon the Earth, and Listen

Lean Down Your Ear
upon the Earth, and Listen

Thomas Wolfe's Greener Modernism

Robert Taylor Ensign

University of South Carolina Press

© 2003 University of South Carolina

Published in Columbia, South Carolina, by the
University of South Carolina Press

Manufactured in the United States of America

07 06 05 04 03   5 4 3 2 1

Library of Congress Cataloging-in-Publication Data

Ensign, Robert Taylor, 1951–
    Lean down your ear upon the earth, and listen : Thomas Wolfe's greener
modernism / Robert Taylor Ensign.
        p. cm.
    Includes bibliographical references and index.
    ISBN 1-57003-481-8 (alk. paper)   ·
    1. Wolfe, Thomas, 1900–1938—Criticism and interpretation. 2. Wolfe, Thomas,
1900–1938—Knowledge—Natural history. 3. Modernism (Literature)—United
States. 4. Ecology in literature. 5. Nature in literature.
    I. Title.
PS3545.O337 Z675 2003
813'.54—dc21

2002010916

For Jill

Contents

Preface

Next to nature herself, my mother, Jill Ensign, who died in 1977, was the most influential source in shaping my appreciation of the natural world. Her enjoyment of the wildness of nature was especially infectious. We spent summers at Big Wolf Lake in the Adirondacks, and I remember how much she loved to witness a mountain rainstorm stealing across the darkened, white-capped waters of our bay. The howling sounds in the trees; the livid and shuddering undersides of birch leaves; the lowering skies; the misty and billowing veil of hard rain; the racing clouds; all filled her with child-like anticipation. I also remember her wading up a creek in old tennis shoes (arthritic feet and all), raptly listening to birdsong at dusk, and rowing me along a shoreline in the early morning as I trolled for fish, with only the squeaky sounds of the oarlocks to punctuate the quiet. It is telling then, that when I wrote a retrospective on my young life at twenty-three, it was bound together mostly by scenes where nature was present:

> He was sensitive to his own sounds as he trudged through the forest. Gradually, his perception of nearness & farness was confused by the shifting dapples underfoot & the kaleidoscopic play of sunlight in the patchwork of leaves. The leaves that were not merely above him, but all around him. And he thought how, in certain evanescent, yet frightening moments, the sight of sunlight in the wash of green would induce a sense of disorientation. As if he were unreal, outside of his body: etherialized into color.

Subsequently, this love of nature found its complement in Thomas Wolfe and his novels. What I discovered was that the natural world casts a vast, green shade over his narratives like an overarching tree. Paradoxically, nature's presence is so ubiquitous in his texts, and Wolfe's romantic descriptions of mountains, rivers, winds, and clouds draw so much attention to themselves as rhetorical tours de force, that it is easy to overlook the extent to which the dramatic action in a Wolfe novel virtually inhabits, and is inseparably bound with, the nonhuman world. With Wolfe, you can miss the forest for the trees.

I live just outside of Portland, Oregon, today and periodically leave my suburban apartment to seek refuge in the many hiking trails that flank the Columbia River. I'm reminded that Wolfe visited this region in the last summer of his life, and I can't help feeling that he would have enjoyed my day trips as much as I do. However, while Wolfe loved nature, he didn't really look the part. When you look at the photos of him on his national parks tour in 1938, he is always dressed in a dark suit, with tie, and appears clumsy and stilted in his poses, as if this son of Appalachia were out of place in a natural setting—another one of those Wolfean contradictions. Still, the measure of his faith in the green world is inscribed in his writing, and while the city matched his intensity, it was nature that gave him back his sanity, as it gives back mine to me.

So, whenever I look down on the Columbia from some rocky height in the Gorge, I like to think Wolfe—a lover of both literal and figurative rivers—is there with me in spirit as well, as, together, we witness that grand river flowing by us, by us, by us, to the sea.

Abbreviations

A	*Antaeus or A Memory of Earth*
CSS	*The Complete Short Stories of Thomas Wolfe*
FDTM	*From Death to Morning*
HB	*The Hills Beyond*
HD	*The Hound of Darkness*
LHA	*Look Homeward, Angel*
LTM	*The Letters of Thomas Wolfe to His Mother*
LTW	*The Letters of Thomas Wolfe*
MOL	*My Other Loneliness: Letters of Thomas Wolfe and Aline Bernstein*
NB	*The Notebooks of Thomas Wolfe*
OTR	*Of Time and the River*
SN	*The Story of a Novel*
WR	*The Web and the Rock*
YCGHA	*You Can't Go Home Again*

Chapter One

Earth-Based Texts

Writing Nature His Way

At first sight, no one is likely to confuse Thomas Wolfe with those writers who form the American canon of nature writing, from Bartram and Thoreau to Berry and Dillard. Moreover, Wolfe's texts are neither nature-oriented nonfiction (such as *Walden*) nor fiction where nature obtrudes dramatically on the action (such as *Moby Dick* and *The Old Man and the Sea*), but rather, works of fiction which incorporate nature but are not ostensibly *about* nature. However, while nature is not Wolfe's subject per se, its pervasive and integral presence throughout his narratives suggests that he tended to conceive human dramas in the broader context of the nonhuman world. Not only do his works reflect an eco-consciousness which seems as palpable and compelling as that of any nature writer, but his treatment of nature also places him in a romantic tradition of American literature, a tradition which predates the modern industrialization of America and conceives the landscape as the omnipresent and ubiquitous medium for all human dramas.

Still, despite his nature-based overview of human existence and the fact that his texts are richly laden with references to the natural world, there have been few studies of his fiction whose sole purpose has been to address the roles and functions of the nonhuman world in his texts. This study seeks to correct this oversight by offering the first in-depth examination of Thomas Wolfe's treatment of nature. It also represents the first time an eco-critical perspective has been applied to his fiction as a whole. Whereas the more common and broadly-used perspectives on literature are anthropocentric and, therefore, address the human aspects of a text while giving minimal or no attention to the nonhuman elements, an ecocritical perspective treats the nonhuman world in fiction as serious a subject for study as the human world. In fact, ecocriticism, "the study of the relationship between literature and the physical environment" (Glotfelty, introduction to *The Ecocriticism Reader,* xviii), treats human and nonhuman life as co-related in an ecological and dynamic relationship. At the same time, this eco-based stance views nature, also referred to here as the "green" world, as the supra-environment that encompasses all others, including human-made habitats. In ecocritical parlance, the term "green" also denotes anything that is imbued with nature, or any text or writer which manifests a compelling awareness of the physical world. Wolfe, it turns out, was greener than we thought, both in his writing and in his outlook, and his romantic orientation reflects this.

While the romantic aspects of Wolfe's writing are apparent throughout his oeuvre, whether in the context of nature or not, they are especially salient when he represents the natural world. For Wolfe, as for the British romantic poets of the nineteenth century, nature best embodies the spirit and letter of romantic ideology. Wolfe's romanticism also ensured that at a time of modernism's preeminence in the arts, his writing of nature would be viewed as both anomalous and self-indulgent. In fact, his handling of nature is markedly different—more emotional, subjective, intense, affirmative, and more engaged—from that of his contemporaries in fiction and poetry, especially the high modernists and socially and politically conscious writers of the 1920s and 1930s; and, consequently, his protagonists experience a different natural—and, therefore, modernist—world altogether. At the same time, Wolfe confounds any neat categorization of his representation of nature by integrating his romanticized mountains, trees, and winds into a modernist narrative space. Moreover, Wolfe demonstrates that modernist issues and themes are not incompatible with protagonists who respond with unmodernist emotional intensity to their surroundings and, in the case of the organic world, draw hope and vitality from them as well. It is important to add, however, that whereas inorganic environments embodied, for Wolfe, different properties and qualities than organic ones, he viewed both types of surroundings from a green perspective. Finally, the anomalous character of Wolfe's environmentalism, especially its conjoining of modernist and romantic elements, is consonant not only with his philosophical outlook, but also with his equally ill-fitting public persona and writing ideology, and any thorough appreciation of his treatment of the natural world must take into consideration these personal and literary contexts.

One of the distinctive aspects of Wolfe's treatment of the nonhuman world is his tendency to conceive it in terms of opposites, a methodology which is congruent with the contradictory nature of his conduct and beliefs. It has been observed that Wolfe was loyal to a fault, yet he cruelly rejected those whom he suspected of disloyalty. He was very sociable, yet he sought a hermitic lifestyle. He eschewed political and social movements, yet he grew to become intensely concerned about political and social corruption and the evils of fascism. He evinced anti-Semitic sentiments, yet the greatest love of his life, Aline Bernstein, was Jewish. He saw human beings as pitiful ciphers in the cosmic void, yet he celebrated the grandeur of humanity's efforts in the spirit and tradition of the Greek tragedians. He abhorred what he viewed as the corrosive materialism of American society and the gap between the rich and the poor, yet he was loyal to America's populist and egalitarian legacy. He demonstrated perspicacity in "reading" human character and physical environments, yet he could so grossly misread others' intentions toward him that he would become paranoid. He felt contempt for the South's romanticization of itself, yet he felt loyal to his southern heritage. He loved the excitement of the great cities of the North, yet he felt drowned in their tumultuous tides. He dissociated himself from literary collectives, yet he befriended individual writers such as F. Scott Fitzgerald and Sinclair Lewis. He loved his editor, Maxwell Perkins, yet he needed to distance himself from him to assert his own independence.

While the quirkiness and shifting moods of Wolfe's personality made him a colorful and enigmatic figure in American letters, it was his size which sowed his folk tale image as a "giant" who tended toward excess in everything he did. As John L. Idol Jr. observes,

> In many of these accounts, he stands as a kind of American giant, a tall man who wrote on top of a refrigerator, drank gallons of coffee or booze a day, ate steaks and chops like they were jelly beans, whored after hundreds of women at home and abroad, carried his manuscripts to his publishers in a truck and took the parts cut out of them home in large taxicabs, held the floor for hours when he talked with people at dinners or parties, engaged in emotional outbursts like a lion roaring, and fell into fits of laughter, most often after telling one of his own adventures. (*A Thomas Wolfe Companion*, 63)

As a result of his persona being writ so large in the eyes of the public, his size was treated by the critics as a metaphor for his artistic excesses as well, and, in fact, the initial critical discourse about Wolfe often conflated the art with the artist. Thus, his characters were either true-to-life or oversized, his language either rhapsodic or overblown, and his emotionalism either poignant or overdone. Accordingly, his detractors often viewed both the writer and his writing as "adolescent." His southern detractors, in particular, noted pejoratively his yokel image, rampant emotionalism, subjective point of view, and autobiographical approach (Rubin, "Thomas Wolfe and the Place He Came From," 200).

In general, Wolfe was perceived by the critical community as either an eloquent writer to be accepted on his own literary and personal terms or an inelegant writer whose organizational structure and prose style testified to his immature development. Detractors cited his formlessness, lack of artistic control, unrestrained emotionalism and verbiage, overwrought language, and overly subjective and autobiographical point of view, while supporters championed his intensity and emotionalism, poetic sensibility, vivid characterizations, sensual imagery, descriptive genius, vision, and lyricism. These opposing responses could be called "formalist" and "lyricist," the pivotal distinction being whether or not Wolfe's linguistic virtuosity was viewed as having transcended his structural flaws. The result was that the reviews of his texts enacted an ongoing polemic over style versus form.[1] Whereas the formalists generally played up the excesses and structural deficiencies of Wolfe's prose, the lyricists generally played them down, claiming that it was a disservice to try to fit Wolfe's oeuvre into conventional genres or that his poetic and dithyrambic language and the depth and evocativeness of his descriptions were their own raison d'etre, all other Wolfean flaws notwithstanding.[2]

Kenneth Brown suggests that the southern critics were not alone in recoiling from Wolfe's backwoods image, and that his personality and conduct were at times akin to a fractious bull in the literary china closet of the 1930s:

> Critics have well-developed ideas about how novels should be written and are not necessarily either liberal or tolerant. Their orientation is commonly toward poise and form and a rather orthodox sophistication that may accept all sorts of irregularities and improprieties of action and speech but cannot abide the bumpkin. And Wolfe struck many as that. He was not merely callow or ingenuous; he came on with a visceral aggressiveness and a disrespect that must have sent some of his critics

scurrying over their vocabularies in search of adequate expression of their disgust. ("Thomas Wolfe—A Critical Visit," 45)

One such critic was Bernard DeVoto, whose denunciation of Wolfe's oeuvre in his legendary review, "Genius Is Not Enough" (1936), best exemplifies the reaction of many of the nominally dispassionate formalists. The pretext for this review in the *Saturday Review of Literature* was the release of Wolfe's *The Story of a Novel* (1936), the chronicle of his struggle to write *Of Time and the River* (1935) and his debt to Maxwell Perkins, his editor at Scribners, for helping him to shape his manuscript. DeVoto's method is to seize on Wolfe's revelations about his writing process to reprove him for various literary juvenilities in *Look Homeward, Angel* (1929) and *Of Time and the River*.[3] For example, after noting Wolfe's sometimes eloquent handling of characters and dramatic scenes in *Look Homeward, Angel,* he notes, "But also there were parts that looked very dubious indeed—long, whirling discharges of words, unabsorbed in the novel . . . badly if not altogether unacceptably written, raw gobs of emotion, aimless and quite meaningless jabber, claptrap, belches, grunts, and Tarzanlike screams" (90). In citing the "rawness" and "unshaped quality" of the writing ("it was as if the birth of the novel had been accompanied by a lot of the material that had nourished its gestation. The material which nature and most novelists discard when its use has been served"), he speculates that such traits either indicate the ineffectual efforts of a literary poseur or constitute "a document in psychic disintegration." DeVoto views *Of Time and the River* as a further falling-off, especially faulting Wolfe for the "giantism" of his characters and his tendency to portray all events as having equal significance. DeVoto saves his most scathing comments, however, for his judgments on Wolfe's lack of artistic control. Using Wolfe's own self-report in *The Story of a Novel* as damning evidence, DeVoto claims that Wolfe cannot be considered a complete artist because he has relied too heavily on Perkins and "the assembly line at Scribners'" (93) to bring order to his literary chaos. Wolfe is, he implies, an artist still in the apprentice stage, lacking the "simple competence in the use of tools" (94) with which to coherently organize his material. Having fostered the image of Wolfe as a callow person and writer, DeVoto's parting advice is that Wolfe needs to rein in both his emotions and his verbiage: "In order to be a great novelist he must also mature his emotions till he can see more profoundly into character than he now does, and he must learn to put a corset on his prose."

The evidence is that Wolfe's refusal to conform to the prevailing literary aesthetics of his era served not only to displease his detractors, but in many cases to antagonize them as well. Moreover, his autobiographical method only encouraged them to address their dislike directly to the author. What is less obvious is why Wolfe's detractors were so vociferous and, at times, even splenetic in their denunciations. Although there is no definitive answer to this, one might speculate that his literary excesses were seen as being so grandiose in scope that his work acted as a literary lightning rod, a fillip to the guardians of both modern and genteel writing.

Despite the pyrotechnics of Wolfe's initial detractors, Wolfe criticism gradually evolved toward being more moderate in tone and less personal in nature.[4] However, despite positive reevaluations of his work by scholars, his inclusion among anthologized southern writers, and references to his texts in studies of the city in American fiction, the literary establishment has persisted in viewing Wolfe's art with a jaundiced eye, thus historicizing him with an asterisk. This treatment is especially well illustrated by the critics' skeptical view of his modernist credentials, a view based on the narrow evidence of his unmodern prose style, the result of which is that Wolfe is never mentioned under the rubric of "modernism" in literary histories of his era. In fact, Wolfe's prose contravened the rules of rhetoric which governed modernist fiction writing in the 1920s and 1930s. The lyricism, verbal excesses, emotional intensity, and personal nature of his writing represented a discordant paean amid the prevailing "dirge" of arid diction, lean passages, restrained emotionalism, and impersonal detachment, all of which comprised the signature of modernist writing. As a result, his writing style was initially viewed as being more a throwback to earlier centuries and writers than a form of early twentieth-century modern prose.[5] In effect, his writing was perceived as neither modernist nor orthodox for the times.[6] Wolfe further distinguished himself from the "sanctioned" modernists by viewing life as backlit by faith rather than fatalism. Even as he and his texts came to express more incisive social criticism, he ultimately parted from his socialist critics (whose sensibilities dominated the critical conversation in the ideological 1930s) by maintaining faith in America's redemptive possibilities.

Despite this legacy of prose-centered criticism, scholars have succeeded in exposing modernist influences and methods in not only Wolfe's novels, but in his short stories and short novels as well. At the same time, any discussion of Wolfe's modernism has traditionally been limited to noting how his writing was influenced by, or merely duplicates, the writing of the *canonical* modernists. For example, scholars have especially noted the Joycean influences and effects in *Look Homeward, Angel* and *The Web and the Rock* (see especially Claire A. Culleton's "Joycean Synchronicity in *Wolfe's Look Homeward, Angel*"; B. R. McElderry Jr.'s *Thomas Wolfe*; Jimmie Carol Still Durr's "*Look Homeward, Angel*, Thomas Wolfe's *Ulysses*"; and Randy W. Oakes's "Myth and Method: Eliot, Joyce, and Wolfe in *The Web and the Rock*"). Whereas Wolfe's admiration for Joyce was unquestioned, he felt ambivalent toward T. S. Eliot, a stance which is reflected in the fact that while he acknowledged Eliot's stature and modernist influence, he satirized his attitude toward life, America, and art.[7]

As a result of the perception that Wolfe's "modernism" is simply a borrowed form of Joyce-ism, most critics have tended to view Wolfe as a modernist imitator only, thereby overlooking his own innovations and dismissing any suggestion that he be viewed as a legitimate modernist writer on his own terms.[8] In fact, while Wolfe, as with so many of his contemporaries, was strongly influenced by the modernist trend-setting of Joyce and Eliot, his experimental writing represents his own creative and individualistic application of modernist compositional theory and praxis. Thus, he experimented with his own versions of Joyce's epiphanies, Dos Passos' use of cinematic and montage techniques, Eliot's wasteland images, and other modernist methodological trademarks which were in circulation at the time of his writing.[9] Joseph Bentz argues in "The Influence of Modernist Structure in the Short Fiction of Thomas Wolfe" that critics have historically used a double standard in their evaluations of Wolfe's experimentalism: "When Wolfe rejects a traditional plot story for a more experimental approach, his work is called 'formless'; when his contemporaries such as Sherwood Anderson engage in similar experiments, it is called 'modernism'" (150). Tellingly, what has also been obscured by the modernist critical focus on Wolfe's unmodern language and putative formlessness is the fact that he addressed a range of modernist issues and themes, including alienation and fragmentation, the bankruptcy of social conventions and institutions, the interpersonal gulf between men and women, and cultural decay.

Wolfe's cachet as a modernist is that while his treatment of modernist themes and use of innovative narrative forms and rhetorical effects place him in the very mainstream of modernist experimentation, he was neither modernist in his writing style nor in his outlook toward America and the human condition. Given that both his language and affirmative visions were incongruent with the prevailing trends in both literature and criticism, it is not surprising to discover that his treatment of natural and constructed environments is markedly different from that of his modernist contemporaries. Ultimately, Wolfe's anomalous treatment of environments represents his individual variation on the emerging, dominant paradigms of postwar literature.

The studies of Wolfe's fictional environments may be loosely divided under the rubrics of "place" and "nature."[10] While these studies aptly demonstrate, through Wolfe's life and writing, the acuteness of his environmental consciousness, the extent to which he was affected by his surroundings, and his valuation of the earth, they are generally not framed within an environmental context nor approached from an ecocritical point of view.[11] Moreover, while there have been numerous studies of Wolfe's treatment of place, there have been very few self-contained studies of his treatment of the natural world; it has rarely been a topic unto itself, and when it has been addressed at all, the focus has been more on Wolfe's nature tropes than on his nature consciousness. The result is that while the critical literature *is* richly sown, in a myriad of topical contexts, with insightful observations about Wolfe's use of nature to convey humanist themes and create figurative and rhetorical effects, there has been little discussion of what his treatment of nature suggests about his vision of the natural world.[12]

It is also the case that Wolfe's celebrated prose style (and the polemics over its aesthetic merits) has itself contributed to the critical oversight of his environmental attitude toward nature by drawing more attention to his nature language than his nature thinking. This historically circumscribed inquiry into the subject of Wolfe and nature was initially fostered by the Wolfean "lyricists" of the 1940s, who mistakenly treated his more lyrical references to nature—being more "pastoralized," salient, and compelling than the less lyrical allusions—as representing his only window on the nonhuman world, a univocal perspective which serves to "aesthetize" any discussion which addresses or draws on his treatment of nature. Being indifferent to Wolfe's ideological allegiances, the lyricists treated the art of his language as their textual conversation piece. A case in point is the collection of Wolfean poetic passages, *A Stone, a Leaf, a Door* (1945), where John S. Barnes has arranged excerpts from his fiction, many of which address or refer to nature, into self-contained verse pieces, giving the impression of found objects or literary gems excavated from the bedrock of Wolfean prose. The following two "stanzas" are lifted from *Look Homeward, Angel* and titled, "The Proud Stars":

> It was sunset.
> The sun's vast rim, blood-red,
> Rested upon the western earth,
> In a great field of murky pollen.
> It sank beyond the western ranges.
>
> The clear sweet air was washed
> With gold and pearl.
> The vast hills melted
> Into purple solitudes:
> They were like Canaan and rich grapes.
> (112)

This and other similarly impressionistic passages not only constitute a biased and delimited sampling of Wolfe's references to nature, but also unintentionally serve to trivialize his apprehension of the nonhuman world as being strictly "scenic" in scope and depth. The following comments by Joseph Warren Beach, written in 1941 and addressing the power of Wolfe's sensual imagery, further exemplify this aesthetic reading of Wolfe and nature:

> In [Wolfe's] appeal to the senses, it is not so much the thing itself as the idea of the thing that intrigues him. . . . And this applies, *a fortiori,* to landscapes and seasons, the beauty of nature and the physiognomy of the earth, all more lavishly presented than in any other contemporary novelist and in a vastly more extravagant vein of poetry. No one has written more eloquently of mountains, of summer sunrise in a garden, of French cities and the English countryside, and of the "grand and casual landscapes of America." (*American Fiction: 1920–1940*, 210)

Beach's approach is to view Wolfe's constructions of nature more as eloquent abstractions than as reflections of either an actual, concrete environment or of an overall green vision. In fact, the most popular of

Wolfe's so-called "nature passages" have not only tended to be the more lyrical descriptions, but, as Beach suggests, also the more impressionistic ones ("the idea of the thing"). Thus, while the modernist critics have rejected Wolfe's romantic rhetoric, the lyricists have celebrated it while similarly overlooking what it might indicate about Wolfe's view of the relationship between human beings and the nonhuman world. While Wolfe's oeuvre *is* replete with impressionistic references to nature, they must be seen in the context of Wolfe's overarching green outlook if they are not to be treated as merely aesthetic devices.

Aside from the fixation with Wolfe's nature *rhetoric,* the other reason why the critical treatment of Wolfe and nature has generally been addressed within a literary rather than an environmental purview is that the critical community has historically viewed nature passages as expressing or reflecting humanistic rather than environmental sentiments. While fictional landscapes have been addressed for years as part of literary studies, they have only recently been addressed from an ecocritical point of view. In fact, the critical community's historically non-ecocritical approach to nature may be attributed, at least in part, to the same lack of suitable theoretical and linguistic tools that has traditionally characterized the critical treatment of place and region. Thus, Michael Kowalewski notes,

> Though less charitable explanations are possible, region may be condescended to by critics or simply ignored as a category because many of them simply lack a vocabulary with which to ask engaging philosophical, psychological, or aesthetic questions about what it means to dwell in a place, whether actually or imaginatively. ("Writing in Place: The New American Regionalism," 174)

In claiming that "the modern understanding of how environmental representation works has been derived from the study of the fictive genres rather than nonfiction" (*The Environmental Imagination,* 84), Lawrence Buell asserts that the very language we use to discuss fiction devalues the environment, not only as a fictional subject, but as a fictional element as well. As evidence, Buell points to the flat, stagey connotations of the term "setting," which has long been used in fiction studies to characterize the nonhuman environment. While this term need not be applied so restrictively, its traditional use in reference to nature "deprecates what it denotes, implying that the physical environment serves for artistic purposes merely as backdrop, ancillary to the main event" (85). In fact, only recently has ecocriticism offered an ecological theory, perspective, method, and language for evaluating the significance and meaning of nature in texts from an earth-centered—as opposed to a strictly humanist or human-centered—perspective. This conceptual and linguistic "lag" by critics and non-critics alike reflects society's persistent and historical stance that nature is separate from the human community. In his book, *The Social Creation of Nature* (1992), Neil Evernden traces the evolution of this perception of nature as an alien dimension: "The creation of the word 'nature' engendered an apparent dualism in the world: all is nature or not-nature. And since the 'not-nature' has come to mean essentially 'humanity,' our relationship to nature has seemed equivocal" (84). As a corrective for this artificial schism, ecocriticism treats literature's scope as coterminous with nature. In distinguishing this broader context for literary criticism, Cheryll Glotfelty observes, "In most literary theory 'the world' is synonymous with society—the social sphere. Ecocriticism expands the notion of 'the world' to include the entire ecosphere" (xix). As a result, this more expansive perspective provides a methodological bridge between the human and the nonhuman in texts:

> Ecocriticism takes as its subject the interconnections between nature and culture, specifically the cultural artifacts of language and literature. As a critical stance, it has one foot in literature and the other on land; as a theoretical discourse, it negotiates between the human and the nonhuman. (xix)

It is this perspective and methodology that enables us to "see" more clearly the green dimensions of Wolfe's fiction. While the critical treatment of Wolfe and nature has historically been tantamount to celebrating Wolfe's prose style, and, conversely, the critical treatment of Wolfe's poetry has so often been tantamount to celebrating Wolfe's "nature passages," an ecocritical approach reveals that even Wolfe's lyrical and impressionistic references to nature—"Spring lay abroad through all the garden of this world" (*LHA*, 160)—constitute more than a collection of leitmotifs; rather, they combine with his non-lyrical, yet ubiquitous references to the nonhuman world to form, web-like, an ecological presence in and around the lives of his characters. One can browse through not only the poetic passages contained in *A Stone, a Leaf, a Door* and *The Face of a Nation* (1939), but his major novels as well, to see that even when Wolfe is writing about something other than nature, he taps nature as his most useable and fundamental language: "he is a wave whose power explodes in lost mid-oceans under timeless skies" (*OTR*, 454–55). Nature provides Wolfe with his universal grammar, a grammar with which he is able to write passionately and knowingly about everybody and everything.

In "Speaking a Word for Nature" (1987), Scott Russell Sanders points out that the presence of nature has been a defining aspect of American literature for most of its history: "Again and again in the great works of American literature, the human world is set against the overarching background of nature" (649). Moreover, this background is represented as an active agent in the lives of human beings: "this landscape is no mere scenery, no flimsy stage set, but rather the energizing *medium* from which human lives emerge and by which those lives are bounded and measured" (649). Ann Douglas invokes this same energizing medium in characterizing the distinctive vitality of American literature: "Vitality, not verisimilitude, is the criterion of classic American literature; it offers a portrait of energy itself, of the adrenaline of the psyche, a portrait in which the external landscape is never separate from the landscape within" (*Terrible Honesty: Mongrel Manhattan in the 1920s*, 209). Despite this American tradition in literature, Sanders, among other critics, has noted how fictional texts have evolved toward portraying human affairs apart from nature, as if they were being enacted in some rarefied bell jar outside the natural world:

> Such fiction treats some "little morality play" as the whole of reality, and never turns outward to acknowledge the "wilderness raging round." And by wilderness I mean quite literally the untrammeled being of nature. . . . What is missing from recent fiction, I feel, is any sense of nature, any acknowledgement of a nonhuman context. (649)

John Hay expresses similar sentiments when he claims in the preface to *Nature* (1987), "We give the novelists charge of our demented psyches, our quirks and foibles, but the depth of human character seldom seems anchored in the known earth and its surrounding waters. Man is still on one side, Nature on the other" (10). The result is that American literature has become detached from its "roots."

A counterforce to this trend, however, has been emerging since the 1960s, as various writers, scholars, and critics have been reasserting the

value of nonhuman life and nonhuman contexts in literature and, ultimately, treating humankind in the context of the natural world. Glen Love
points out that western American literature and latter-day nature writing
have both been primary contributors to this movement to reclaim the
physical world in literature and to relocate human beings within it
("Revaluing Nature," 212). Concomitantly, ecocriticism has emerged to
legitimate not only this movement, its literature, and any literature which
conveys a valuation of nature, but also ecocentric readings of *all* literature.
As a result of these combined efforts in both criticism and literature, nature
is now being treated in texts as a meaningful narrative agent with its own
integrity rather than as a rhetorical ornament or "blank" backdrop. Thus,
a perspective which predated the modern industrialization of America—
conceiving the landscape as an "energizing medium"—is now being used
by contemporary writers and critics to conceptualize human existence as
human beings living with and within nature.

While Wolfe's narratives are similarly eco-based, it has not been fully
appreciated how the natural world serves as the overriding medium for his
stories. While he is ostensibly the most anthropocentric of authors, he
nevertheless viewed humanity as living both within and under the aegis of
nature, and, accordingly, his literary focus on human life is constantly
qualified by his references and allusions to the natural world. Thus, his
protagonists are seen not only to be "grounded" in their environments in
general, and ultimately grounded in nature, but to be interpenetrated and
encompassed by nature as well.

While Wolfe apprehended both nature and human-made environments
from an ecological perspective, he valued and respected nature more, a
stance which reflected his view that nature—being not only a physical
dimension, but a cosmic and spiritual one as well—transcends humankind
and its artifacts. This qualitative difference is implicit in the following
comments he made in his notebook (July 14, 1930) while touring Switzer-
land: "went to Champéry this afternoon—the inevitable mountains—a
steepness, a depth, an eternity that is indescribable. Why is it that the vastness of nature never humiliates one, but the vastness of a city does? This is
true" (*NB*, vol. 2, 481). In reflecting this view, Wolfean nature retains its
inviolability throughout his works despite his protagonists' feelings of
angst, fear, and even terror when confronted with the nonhuman world's
seeming indifference. Moreover, Wolfe treated nature's integrity and overall presence as a reassuring source of constancy, and, as a result, used the

natural world as an anchor for both the structure and the content of his narratives; thus, it not only provides structural coherence for his texts, but also a narrative "still point"—a source of balance, stability, and sanity—in the otherwise unstable world and lives of his protagonists. In Wolfe's modernist fictional world, there is a saving green amid the wasteland.

Chapter Two

The Environmental Relationship

Ecological and Personal

While Wolfe viewed nature as qualitatively different from constructed environments, he wrote both human and nonhuman surroundings according to the same processes of apprehension and composition, as well as drawing on the same beliefs, attitudes, and values about the place of environments in human lives. Moreover, if environmentally conscious writers are those who readily negotiate between human consciousness and environmental phenomena in their texts, and if the locus of this negotiation is language, it is self-evident that Wolfe most distinguishes himself from his contemporaries—as a writer in general and an environmentalist in particular—through his language. If, therefore, understanding the anomalous character of his fictional environments is inseparable from understanding the anomalous character of his language, comparing his prose style to the prevailing discourse in fiction during the 1920s and 1930s is the fundamental starting point for any discussion of Wolfe's handling of natural and constructed environments in his texts.

Most modernist fiction writers tended, in principle, to distrust narrators who seemed either "too" subjective or "too" emotional. The government's hypocritical prosecution of World War One in the media had dramatized for them the deceitful possibilities of language and, combined with their desire to overturn the genteel writing and temperament which still dominated American letters in the early part of the twentieth century, they responded by pledging to write "objectively," to write "true." Given this injunction, any demonstrations of emotional excess or overwrought prose were viewed as risking the sentimentalization—and, therefore, the distortion or subversion—of the "truth." Prettified language was not to be trusted; romantic ideology and cant were the currency of falsehoods. Similarly, subjective points of view were considered myopic and self-indulgent. As a result, constrained and "sober" prose—lean diction, lean sentences, and journalistic detachment—was the predominant mode of literary expression, and this discourse was viewed by most modernist novelists as being best suited for making critical appraisals of postwar culture. Given this ideology, the environment, viewed as no less a cultural artifact than anything else, was treated primarily as a discursive space for "truth-telling"; that is, it was of interest less for itself than for how it might be used, rhetorically, to comment on social, economic, and political conditions. Given that the modernist temper and outlook tended toward cynicism and a jaded vision of western culture, this translated into landscapes—both natural and human-made—which were either superficial, denatured, benighted, emotionally flat, oppressive, devitalized, or static. In *The Great Gatsby,* Fitzgerald suggests that the frontier image of America as "the fresh, green breast of the new world" has been bankrupt for a long time; both the landscape and its people have lost their integrity, and the prospect of redemption is remote (189). Thus, the valley of ashes, a literal wasteland, ultimately symbolizes the detritus of Fitzgerald's bright hopes for the American scene. Similarly, Hemingway's blighted landscapes in *In Our Time,* the ruins of the old mill in "The End of Something," and the fire-scarred hill in "Big Two-Hearted River" are metaphors for the author's vision of a cultural landscape of loss and decay. While the namesake river in the latter story represents a medium for renewal, it appears tragic rather than celebratory due to its solitariness amid the surrounding wasteland.

Although Wolfe shared the same desire to write true, his vision of the truth and his aesthetic philosophy were different from those of his contemporaries and, therefore, required different rules of rhetoric. Wolfe's language became especially keyed to his effort to communicate his own vision of America, and, to a great extent, to study the art of Wolfe's treatment of the environment is to study his portrait of America as a geographic place best transcribed in idioms that are indigenous to it, sprung from its earth and cultural compost:

> Out of the billion forms of America, out of the savage violence and the dense complexity of all its swarming life; from the unique and single substance of this land and life of ours, must we draw the power and energy of our own life, the articulation of our speech, the substance of our art. (*SN,* 93)[1]

Wolfe came to believe that his own writing embodied this mythical American argot and ethos, and in a letter to Maxwell Perkins (November, 1936), he announced his readiness to articulate his America: "Like Mr. Joyce, I have at last discovered my own America, I believe I have found my language, I think I know my way. And I shall wreak out my vision of this life, this way, this world and this America, to the top of my bent" (*LTW*, 587).[2]

Wolfe constructed a personalized, subjectivist rhetoric which reflected his sensual and passionate nature, and which was embodied in a vital style characterized by lyricism, verbal excess, and emotional intensity. Whereas Stein inveighed against nouns and adjectives, and the Imagists decried superfluous verbiage, Wolfe not only used nouns in endless lists and adjectives in endless series, but also released his emotions in lengthy rhetorical passages which seem to celebrate the sounds and pageantry of language itself. While his contemporaries subscribed to an aesthetic ideology of restraint (especially of verbiage and emotion), Wolfe, who had adopted Coleridge's organic model for composition (a model which mirrored Wolfe's organic vision of life), refused to be bound by the literary dicta of the day. Thus, when he asserted, "I shall use as precisely, as truthfully, as tellingly as I can every word I have to use; every word, if need be, in my vocabulary" (*LTW*, 587), he was proclaiming an aesthetic stance that flouted the taciturn style of his contemporaries. Word volume, he believed, should not be governed by ideology-bound rules, but by the demands of the writing situation; therefore, to write "precisely" was not to write economically but to tell the "truth" in however many words—and with whatever type of words—were necessary. Given this literary license to write without restraint—"There has never been a time when I've been so determined to write as I please" (584)—Wolfe was willing to submit to Perkins's editorial scalpel only up to a certain point; above all, the voice and spirit of the "outsider" from Appalachia must remain free:

> But let us not get the issues confused, let us not again get into the old confusion between substance and technique, purpose and manner, direction and means, the spirit and the letter. Restrain my adjectives, by all means, discipline my adverbs, moderate the technical extravagances of my incondite exuberance, but don't derail the train, don't take the Pacific Limited and switch it down the siding towards Hogwart Junction. It can't be done. I'm not going to let it happen. (588)[3]

Not surprisingly, Wolfe's lack of restraint distinguishes not only his prose from that of his contemporaries, but his construction of fictional

environments as well. Most significantly, it serves to charge his environments with greater vitality, an energized presence which reflects the
influence of his own exuberant personality (whose wildness was fueled to
a great extent by his openness to nature's sensory influx), his susceptibility and receptivity to the evocative impact of all environmental phenomena, and his conception of a life force interpenetrating all matter.[4]
The latter was his variation on the formal doctrine of vitalism as popularized by Shaw, H. G. Wells, Nietzsche, and Bergson.[5] This philosophical
doctrine was based on a biological view of life which held vitality as a
supreme value because it was viewed as being part of a pervasive life force
which naturally and ineluctably flows toward greater and more progres-
sive states of being and life. While this doctrine limited its scope to
organic matter, Wolfe applied it to inorganic and inanimate matter as
well. So compelling and seductive was this force for Wolfe that his representations of inanimate matter became kinetic and his human-made
environments organic. Thus, for instance, New York City's Pennsylvania
Station is figured as a living, oceanic bio-system:

> The station, as he entered it, was murmurous with the immense and dis-
> tant sound of time. . . . It had the murmur of a distant sea, the lan-
> guorous lapse and flow of waters on a beach. It was elemental, detached,
> indifferent to the lives of men. They contributed to it as drops of rain
> contribute to a river that draws its flood and movement majestically
> from great depths, out of purple hills at evening. (*YCGHA*, 43)

This imaginative transfiguration of an otherwise drab and commonplace
environment further distinguishes Wolfe's treatment of landscapes from
that of his contemporaries. While Wolfe was able to transcribe his perceptions of environments with great integrity and similitude, his representations—in fiction and nonfiction alike—were characteristically a
combination of objective and subjective impressions.[6] In the special case
of his subjective impressions of urban spaces, his romantic tendency to see
the marvelous in the commonplace produced images—such as organic
train stations—which constituted a challenge to the monolithic, dark
cityscapes which ruled fiction in Wolfe's day.[7]

Wolfe's city, of course, was primarily New York, and he was only one
of many noteworthy American writers (Crane, Whitman, Wharton, Dos
Passos, and James among others) who have been drawn to it as their

literary subject or fictional stage (Kazin, *A Writer's America: Landscape in Literature,* 152–73). In fact, New York City, which Wolfe treated as a metaphor for the nation, has been historically *the* first city of American letters, a city whose paradoxical qualities have also most emblematized American writers' ambivalence toward urban spaces.[8] As Graham Clarke observes:

> Indeed, New York remains a double city. As [Whitman's] Manhattan it retains its mythic promise and remains an image at once familiar and inviting. As [Melville's] New York City it becomes part of a different *urban* process: denied its mythic energy, its transcendent base, it moves into an historical reality in which social, political and economic questions are prominent. It becomes, in other words, a city of people rather than images—of social contingencies rather than mythic projections ("A 'Sublime and Atrocious' Spectacle: New York and the Iconography of Manhattan Island," 39).

Most writers reconciled their ambivalence by embracing Melville's "atrocious" overview while at the same time rejecting the romanticized, "sublime" visions of Whitman (39). By contrast, while Wolfe shared his contemporaries' Melvillean view (especially that of urban fiction writers such as Farrell, Dreiser, and Wright) that America's urban landscape was an anti-humanistic habitat and an icon of cultural decay, his environmental vision was expansive enough to enable him also to see more of Whitman's light in the urban darkness, more affirmative images amid the wasteland. Wolfe's representations of the city are also more protean than those of his contemporaries because they reflect the lability of his emotions and his tendency to apprehend all phenomena in terms of oppositions.[9] Thus, he portrays the city not only as a dynamic place, but also as a kaleidoscopic arena of changing imagery. As a consequence of this variableness, Wolfe's city embodies an incongruous doubleness, as illustrated by George Webber's simultaneously romantic *and* naturalistic vision of New York City:

> It was a cruel city, but it was a lovely one; a savage city, yet it had tenderness; a bitter, harsh, and violent catacomb of stone and steel and tunneled rock, slashed savagely with light, and roaring, fighting a constant warfare of men and of machinery; and yet it was so sweetly and so delicately pulsed, as full of warmth, of passion, and of love, as it was full of hate. (*WR,* 439)[10]

In his oppositional views of the city, his negative, pessimistic visions are keyed to the human landscape, as in the robotic, zombie-like city dwellers who resemble

> living tissue from which all of the radiant and succulent essences of individual character and memory have been extracted—and which flowed constantly back and forth along the beaten pavement in a lava-like tide of tallowy flesh, dark dead eyes, and gray felt hats. The gray felt hats . . . drowned him with their tidal flow of weariness and sterility: they seemed to be the badge, the uniform, of a race of mechanical creatures. (*OTR*, 423)

By contrast, his positive, optimistic visions, which focus on the nonhuman landscape, represent rare affirmative responses to the urban scene, or any other twentieth-century scene, among Wolfe's contemporaries:

> Spring comes up in bright flowers below the feet of April, and below the feet of lovers the earth yields up all its glory and opulence. Therefore they drew up ripeness out of stone and steel, beauty from shambles of old brick. The earth blazed with its potent and imperial colors because they were so fit and equal for it, and because there was no falseness in their hearts. (*WR*, 416)

While Dos Passos shared Wolfe's vision of the city as a dynamic place—which he suggests through the onrushing sense of movement engendered by discontinuous narratives, staccato sentences, and disjunctive news fragments—he generally figures this dynamism in only negative terms. T. S. Eliot, however, envisions the modern city as lacking dynamism altogether. His depiction of the landscape of the 1920s as a "waste land" established a topographical standard against which other writers, novelists as well as poets, measured their own landscape images. In fact, Eliot established the definitive image and tone of the modern city for the writers of his era when he portrayed London, in the "The Waste Land," as a place of the living dead, its landscape fit only for the cultivation of corpses (lines 60–76). By contrast, if Wolfe's negative representations of the city actually outnumber his positive ones—with some of Wolfe's damning visions of New York and Boston even exceeding the hellish images of Eliot's Londonscapes—his distinction lies in the fact that he was still able to salvage redemptive scenes within its benighted landscape. Thus, for Wolfe, *all* of

America was a checkered, yet ultimately incandescent landscape, and while he probed and recorded its dark spaces with a "terrible honesty" (Douglas), his environmental vision also encompasses the optimistic dimension of his writing as well as his investment in locating and liberating the buried light in America's back alleys and back roads.[11]

Ultimately, Wolfe's selective, luminous images of America's landscapes were acts of faith, a faith enunciated by George Webber when he tells his editor, Foxhall Edwards (the Maxwell Perkins persona), "I believe that we are lost here in America, but I believe we shall be found. And this belief, which amounts now to the catharsis of knowledge and conviction, is for me—and I think for all of us—not only our own hope, but America's ever-lasting, living dream" (*YCGHA*, 574). In the meantime, Wolfe gained comfort from his belief in man's ability to stay against his own existential confusion, and he included himself among those who derive meaning and significance from their refusal to surrender to fatalism. Thus, George Webber asserts:

> And the essence of all faith, it seems to me, for such a man as I . . . is that man's life can be, and will be, better; that man's greatest enemies, in the forms in which they now exist—the forms we see on every hand of fear, hatred, slavery, cruelty, poverty, and need—can be conquered and destroyed. (571)

Given this credo, Wolfe eschewed, even derided, the unrelieved pessimism of the "waste-lander," a position he articulates in a letter to Alfred Dashiell (November, 1930):

> If you speak of me to anyone, for God's sake do not communicate any of this letter to people who would use it to mock at and injure me: I mean the futility boys and girls, the stealthy lasses, the elegant mockers, the American T. S. Elioters. They are a low but vilely cunning lot of bastards and they will not see their cheap little stock in trade—I mean the what-is-the-use-we-are-a-doomed-generation, life-here-is-a-barren-desert, we-can-do-nothing—they will not see this little business cursed without hissing and jeering retaliation. (*LTW,* 275)

Although the sanguine aspects of Wolfe's philosophy are not fully articulated until the final novel of his tetralogy, *You Can't Go Home Again* (1940), and while his own pessimism cast splintered shadows throughout his oeuvre, he persisted all along in illuminating the half-concealed gardens of hope and sensual beauty which still bloomed in the wastelander's environmental desert.

Wolfe's representation of American—or any other—landscapes is also distinguished by the fact that whereas his contemporaries tended to use emotionally detached and objective points of view, he used an emotionally engaged and subjective perspective. In effect, it is empirically based (within his fictional world), distilled through the consciousnesses of his primary protagonists, Eugene Gant and George Webber; it is their (subjective) world, and theirs only, that we experience. As a result, Wolfe's representation of contact with environments tends to be more personal and immediate than that of his contemporaries.

It is significant, moreover, that this subjective point of view is conveyed not only via a third person narrator, but also without any loss of subjectivity. This impression is produced by the conflated psyches of the protagonists and narrators, the effects of which are felt more acutely in Wolfe's first two novels than in his last two. Specifically, the narrators identify only with George Webber's or Eugene Gant's point of view, a process of overlapping identification that is fostered by the fact that the narrators' poetic speech seems credibly to "fit" the poetic consciousnesses of the protagonists, both of whom are aesthetes.[12] In the following passage from *Look Homeward, Angel,* the interjection of Eugene's consciousness into the narrator's speech makes this conflation overt: "The cock crew his shrill morning cry of life beginning and awakening. The cock that crew at midnight (thought Eugene) has an elfin ghostly cry. His cry was drugged with sleep and death" (468). Even the rhetorical or apostrophic passages, which appear textually as disjunctive interjections, as well as the narrative scene-setting and observations about environmental phenomena, may be viewed as choric echoes of Eugene's and George's thoughts and feelings. While many rhetorical passages are problematic in terms of their thematic "fit" and sudden shifts in voice, it is still the case that all speakers in Wolfe's texts are anchored in the psyches of the protagonists.

In utilizing this subjective orientation, Wolfe situates his protagonists in a physical, felt, and ecological relationship with their environments, a dynamic which produces scenes where protagonists engage and interact with concrete, steel, earth, sun, flowers, and wind as if they were dramatis personae no less compelling than the human landscape. This environmental stance is an extension of Wolfe's philosophical approach to living fully, of making contact with all phenomena in his sensory field, a field which encompasses city streets, hills, and stars as well as sounds, smells, and people. As James Dickey has observed, Wolfe's was "the vision, projected in everything [he] wrote, of the world as a place for total encounters: a place in which one may *connect* with the objects of life, its people, its events, and mysteries in an absolutely maximum way, to the limit of human capacity" (Foreword to *The Complete Short Stories of Thomas Wolfe*, xiii). Wolfe's editor, Maxwell Perkins, believed that Wolfe's inordinate desire for such encounters was shaped by his "imprisonment" within the mountains surrounding Asheville:

> By this imprisonment, one can think, Tom's imagination was intensified, and his desire for experience, by being pent up, was increased and sharpened. It was not this that made him what he was, of course, but the character of what he did and wrote was qualified by it. This . . . later increased his sense, as with one released from a prison, that there was not enough time, and so made him wild to see, read, taste, feel and record everything. ("Thomas Wolfe: A Writer for the People of His Time and Tomorrow," 3)

Wolfe's alertness to his surroundings, a propensity that could sometimes yield moments of spiritual rhapsody, is dramatized in the following observation by Robert Raynolds, a friend of Wolfe's, as they were walking the streets of New York City:

> Wolfe walked along the street as if his business were right there; his business was to hear, see, feel, taste and touch and smell the life of the street; he was working as he walked. This gave his face an alert, lively expression, animal in its watchfulness, with his wary lower lip thrust out; then from time to time the gatherings of his senses coalesced in a spiritual perception, and the joy of spiritual apprehension lit up his face. (*Thomas Wolfe: Memoir of a Friendship*, 23)

Wolfe's own descriptions of his protagonists' environmental contact similarly serve to illuminate characterological traits. Accordingly, Eugene Gant and George Webber are constantly defined by—and derive much of their character, depth, and substance from—their individualistic responses to constructed and natural surroundings. In fact, Eugene's and George's characteristic responses to the environment afford as viable portraits of themselves as do their interactions with other characters, a dynamic that relies on Wolfe's ability to simulate in his protagonists (and narrators) his own capacity for close engagement with his surroundings.

Wolfe produces this simulated closeness with environments through descriptions of psychic, emotional, and sensory contact, as well as of bodily assimilation. When, for example, he describes George Webber and his uncle "smashing their way through the dry and brittle undergrowth of barren Winter, hearing the dry report of bough and twig beneath their feet, the masty spring and crackle of brown ancient leaves" (WR, 152), he closes the physical and felt distance between the nonhuman world and George's consciousness by using sensual language, the overheard onomatopoeic sounds ("masty spring and crackle") of physical contact with the earth. Sensual language especially mirrors the depth and scope of young Eugene Gant's sensory orientation to the world, as evidenced by his capacious memory:

> Eugene was loose now in the limitless meadows of sensation: his sensory equipment was so complete that at the moment of perception of a single thing, the whole background of color, warmth, odor, sound, taste established itself, so that later, the breath of hot dandelions brought back the grass-warm banks of Spring, a day, a place, the rustling of young leaves, or the page of a book, the thin exotic smell of tangerine, the wintry bite of great apples; or, as with Gulliver's Travels, a bright windy day in March, spurting moments of warmth, the drip and reek of the earth-thaw, the feel of the fire. (LHA, 66)

George Webber's ("Monk") similar capacity for sensory-based recall enables him to distinguish cities according to their characteristic odors:

> Each great city Monk had known had had an odor for him. Boston had an odor in its crooked streets of fresh-ground coffee mixed with smoke. Chicago, when the wind from the West set in, had an unmistakable odor of burning pork. New York was so much harder to define, but he thought it was the odor of electricity, it was the odor of the cellar, of an old brick house or of a city building, closed, a little stale and dank, touched with a subtle, fresh, half-rotten smell of harbor. (WR, 600)

In The Story of a Novel, Wolfe notes, "The quality of my memory is characterized, I believe, in a more than ordinary degree by the intensity of its sense impressions, its power to evoke and bring back the odors, sounds, colors, shapes, and feel of things with concrete vividness" (31).

Wolfe further conveys a sense of closeness with environments by charging his descriptive, contactful language with feelings. Landscapes are, for Wolfe, necessarily emotion-laden, and, as a result, the world "outside" is brought "inside" by being made over in the image of the protagonist's own feelings; thus, an otherwise impersonal world becomes imbued with personal meanings and shades of emotional coloration. The section of *Of Time and the River* where Eugene travels to and from South Carolina not only establishes the protagonist's emotional state by highlighting his perceptions of the environment, but also dramatizes how his different emotions cause him to assimilate different impressions of the same landscape. During the ride down, for example, he is drunk with alcohol and feelings of immortality, and, as a result, his euphoric mood causes his sight to fasten onto those aspects of his surroundings which affirm his emotional state:

> Around them, below them—from the living and shining air of autumn, from the enbrowned autumnal earth, from the great shapes of the hills behind them with their molten mass of color—dull browns, rich bitter reds, dark bronze, and mellow yellow—from the raw crude clay of the piedmont earth and the great brown stubble of the cotton fields—from a thousand impalpable and unutterable things, there came this glorious breath of triumph and delight. It was late October, there was a smell of smoke upon the air, an odor of burning leaves, the barking of a dog, a misty red, pollenated gold in the rich, fading, sorrowful, and exultant light of the day. (366)

During the ride back, however, he is feeling chastened after having been arrested for drunkenness, and, as a result, his emotions now lead him to experience the landscape as a simulacrum of his contrastive, darker mood:

> The ride back up into the hills with Luke was cold, dark, bleak, and desolate—the very painting of his own sick soul. Black night had come when they had reached the mountains. The stars were out, and around them the great bulk of the hills was barren, bleak, and wintry-looking, and there was the distant roaring of demented winds upon the hills, the lonely preludes of grim winter among the barren trees. (396)

As a result of his change in emotions, Eugene is painfully aware of how his felt relationship with the environment has also changed:

> Already, it seemed, the same landscape which only a day or two before had flamed with all the blazing colors of October, and with the enchantment which his hope and joy had given it, had been sorrowfully transformed by the mournful desolation of coming winter. The earth was no longer beautiful and friendly: it had become a waste, a desert, and a prison bleak and bare. (396)

Wolfe's protagonists can also feel close to the environment to the point of bodily assimilation. Thus, Wolfe characterizes Eugene's memories of "the sounds of America" as "the things that are in his blood, his heart, his brain, in every atom of his flesh and tissue" (*OTR*, 859); and, in describing the stimulating effects of New York City on young men, Wolfe writes, "It lays its hand upon a man's bowels" (*WR*, 221). Similarly, Wolfe figures young George Webber's bodily assimilation of winter winds, during his hiking excursions into the mountains with his uncle, Mark Joyner, as a process of ingestion: "he gulped it down into his aching lungs" (152). This bodily assimilation can also extend to bodily identification, such as when, in *Of Time and the River*, Wolfe suggests how the Brooklyn Bridge's architecture is confounded with Eugene Gant's viscera: "What bridge? The bridge whereon at night he had walked and stood and watched a thousand times, until . . . every stone of its twin terrific arches was in his heart" (*OTR*, 536). Wolfe describes his own experience of bodily identification with environments when, in a letter to Alfred Dashiell (November, 1930), he talks about America's natural landscape as if he had given birth to it: "I tell you I know [America] as if it were my child, as if it had been distilled from my blood and marrow: I know it from the look and smell of the railway ties to the thousand sounds and odours of the wilderness" (*LTW*, 273).

Wolfe's representation of contact with the environment is also based on an ecological—interrelational and interdependent—relationship, that is, his notion that our experience of the environment is the product of a dynamic interaction between the weather of our surroundings and the weather of our senses, emotions, bodies, and psyches. By implication, this landscape is also an *evocative* one, as it is for Wolfe throughout his oeuvre. Thus, when the vitality of George Webber's or Eugene Gant's consciousness engages directly with the vitality of the environment, there is an exchange; there is contact. As a result of this interactive dynamic, the vitality of their perceptions and imaginations sometimes overwhelms the vitality of the environment's conditions, a case of mind over matter; and, contrariwise, the environment sometimes overwhelms their psyches.[13] Never, however, is the environment experienced as a static or passive entity. Accordingly, perceptions of surroundings in Wolfe's fictional world are not to be conceived as being exclusively projections, merely reflections of self-consciousness; they are also the products of the evocative impact of surroundings *on* consciousness. This compelling quality of the environment is implicit in Wolfe's description of the London air, a palpable medium which induces effects at the sensory ("The wet, woolen air"), bodily ("the slow movements of the people"), emotional ("his heart is dull"), and psychic ("there is no hope") level:

> the wool-gray air is all about him like a living substance; it is in his heart, his stomach, and his entrails; it is in the slow movements of the people; it soaks down from the sodden skies into the earth, into the heavy buildings, into the limbs and hearts and grains of living men. It soaks into the spirit of the wanderer; his heart is dull with the gray weariness of despair. . . . The wet, woolen air is all about him, and there is no hope. (*OTR*, 860)

Even in the case of Eugene's round trip to South Carolina, the landscape both evokes, and is imbued with, his feelings. Not only does Eugene's mood change from exultation to despondency, but the countryside itself changes from being warm and illuminated to cold and darkened. As a result, the difference in Eugene's emotions and perceptions is the difference between a warm dusk in fall and a cold night in winter. While he had "given" the landscape his "hope and joy" on the ride down, matching its "blazing" presence with his upbeat mood, on the ride back the same landscape becomes "sorrowfully transformed" by both Eugene's "sick soul" and the environment's "barren, bleak, and wintry-looking" presence. Thus, an ecological loop unfolds: while Eugene's emotions shape his perceptions of the land and the weather, the land and weather, conversely, influence the colors, shades, and tones of his emotional palette.[14]

When this interplay between character and surroundings is confluent and affirmative, an energetic synergy can occur and a state of mystical union can result. This rarefied dialogue denotes the highest state of

connectedness with surroundings in a Wolfe text. Eugene experiences this
state when he rides down to South Carolina, and he also experiences it
when his feelings of love for Laura James find their environmental complement in the "timeless valley":

> They lay there, locked together, upon that magic carpet, in that paradise.
> . . . All of that magic world—flower and field and sky and hill, and all the
> sweet woodland cries, sounds and sight and color—grew into him, one
> voice in his heart, one tongue in his brain, harmonious, radiant, and
> whole—a single passionate lyrical noise. (*LHA*, 378)

Such lyrical harmony is possible in an urban setting as well. When Eugene
emerges into the crowded streets of Boston after a talk with old Bascom
Pentland, "the exultancy, the power, [and] the joy that pulsed in [him]"
(149) find their environmental complement in the city's sensual evocations:

> Then the boy got up and left him and went out into the streets where
> the singing and lyrical air, the man-swarm passing in its million-footed
> weft, the glorious women and the girls compacted in a single music of
> belly and breasts and thighs, the sea, the earth, the proud, potent, clam-
> orous city, all of the voices of time, fused to a unity that was like a song,
> a token and a cry. (*OTR*, 149–50)

While Wolfe did not always pitch his environmental descriptions at such
high octaves of intensity and lyricism, he never lost sight of how landscape-making and consciousness-making are bound together.

The environment in Wolfe's texts participates in ecologically shaping
not only feelings and perceptions, but the *self* (and, therefore, "character")
as well. Here, Paul Shepard's articulation of this self formation process is a
useful guide to Wolfe's own ideology and practice. According to Shepard,
"The environment is encountered [during the early stages of self develop-
ment] in a way in which self and place are related" (*Man in the Landscape*,
34). As a result of this psychic mapping, "the organizing of thinking,
perception, and meaning is intimately related to specific places" (34), and
"the territory and the sacred places within it orient the individual to
topography, position him in the land and in the cosmos, an environmental gestalt of figure and ground" (37). Ultimately, the compasses of self and

place become inextricable: "Knowing who you are is impossible without knowing where you are" (Paul Shepard, "Place in American Culture," 32). Operating from these same premises, Wolfe dramatizes the centrality of place in Eugene Gant's originary psychic map of himself and "his" world. Thus, we are told how Eugene's child self is grounded "in" his hometown ("with a child's egotism it was for him the centre of the earth, the small but dynamic core of all life" [LHA, 89]) and "in" the surrounding mountains: "The mountains were his masters. They rimmed in life. They were the cup of reality, beyond growth, beyond struggle and death. They were his absolute unity in the midst of eternal change" (158).

In fact, Wolfe's texts eloquently serve as case studies in how character formation is, to a great extent, the negotiation of a person's orientation to place. Thus, Eugene Gant ponders why people who live in the eastern part of his hometown, which fronts the near hills, are different in character from those from the western part of town, which fronts the distant mountains:

> Here are the boys from the eastern part of town . . . the older, homelier, and for some reason more joyful and confident part of town to him. . . . Perhaps it is because the hills along the eastern borders of the town are near and close and warm, and almost to be touched. But in the western part of town, the great vistas of the soaring ranges, the distant summits of the Smokies fade far away into the west, into the huge loneliness, the haunting desolation of the unknown distance, the red, lonely light of the powerful retreating sun. (OTR, 205)

The implication is that the confidence and joy of the "easterners" derive from their feeling protected by the closeness of the hills, while the loneliness of the "westerners" derives from their feeling alienated by the remoteness of the mountains. Wolfe indicated his awareness of the environment's impact on his own character when he noted, "One half of me is great fields and mighty barns, and one half of me is the great hills of North Carolina" (LTM, 162). Similarly, he saw the Vermont landscape of Max Perkins's childhood etched in his stolid persona:

> While we were sweeping up the Perkins country, down around White River Junction, Tom noticed that more farmhouses than usual were built of brick. These houses looked compact, impregnable, and secure on the ground.

"I might have known Max came from a section like this," he said. "If Vermont is solid, this is the most solid part of it, and he is the most solid Vermonter ever born. . . . Just look at that brick house . . . under those big maples; a hurricane couldn't make it tremble. That's Max." (Raynolds, 99)[15]

Given that Wolfe believed *all* settings are capable of shaping consciousness as well as the self, he treats urban settings as no less influential than rural ones. While many critics have focused on the extent to which his urban images may be read as objective correlatives of Wolfe's own consciousness, thus treating the Wolfean city as a mirror only, a Rorschach of his own mind, few have addressed the extent to which Wolfe depicts urban environments as formative agents of both character and consciousness. In the following passage, city dwellers are treated as urban "offspring" whose characters and psyches are shaped by the volume, cadence, and discords of their surroundings, their life forces drained by the city's febrile syncopation:

The city was their stony-hearted mother, and from her breast they have drawn a bitter nurture. Born to brick and asphalt, to crowded tenements and swarming streets, stunned into sleep as children beneath the sudden slamming racket of the elevated trains, taught to fight, to menace, and to struggle in a world of savage violence and incessant din, they had had the city's qualities stamped into their flesh and movements, distilled through all their tissues, etched with the city's acid into their tongue and brain and vision. Their faces were tough and seamed, the skin thick, dry, without hue of freshness or color. Their pulse beat with the furious rhythm of the city's stroke. (*YCGHA*, 35)

Although Wolfe emphasizes here the depth and scope of the environment's influence and not the imaginative play of individual consciousness on its surroundings, he nevertheless assumed, as William Carlos Williams did, "an / interpenetration, both ways" ("Preface," *Paterson*, 24–25).[16]

Wolfe also believed that the influential effects of place on the psyche are, as Edith Cobb has attested, especially maximal during childhood. The following passage from *The Web and the Rock* not only reflects this view, but also exemplifies Shepard's notion that "space is not infinite, nor homogenous, nor abstract. It is bounded, and emotionally and spiritually diverse: familiar, alien, hostile, friendly" (*Man in the Landscape*, 36):

> His [George Webber's] sense of *place,* the feeling for specific locality that later became so strong in him, came, he thought, from all these associations of his youth—from his overwhelming conviction, or prejudice, that there were "good" places and "bad" ones. . . . By the time he was twelve years old, he had constructed a kind of geography of his universe, composed of these powerful and instinctive affections and dislikes. (*WR*, 18)

This reference to neighborhood-scale places also dramatizes the fact that any study of Wolfe's treatment of place must address not only macro spaces such as the South, New York City, and Appalachia, but also micro spaces—such as Altamont's town square: "He [Gant] felt suddenly the cramped mean fixity of the Square; this was the one fixed spot in a world that writhed, evolved, and changed constantly in his vision" (*LHA*, 62), "it [the Square] was for him [Grover] earth's pivot and the granite core of changelessness" ("The Lost Boy," *CSS*, 359–60). Moreover, similarly compelling spatial attachments can be made to a school ("the school had become the centre of his heart and life" [*LHA*, 192]), a street ("For the place where he lived was not just a street to him—not just a strip of pavement and a design of weathered, shabby houses; it was a living integument of his life, the frame and stage for the whole world of childhood and enchantment" [*WR*, 105]), and even a person: "The woman [Esther Jack] had become a world for him—a kind of new America—and now he lived in it, explored it all the time" (*WR*, 376). The implication is that, for Wolfe, not only all types of environments, but also all scales of environments have equal capacity to shape human consciousness. Moreover, Wolfe's texts suggest that the effects of our attachment to places can last for the rest of our lives, as evidenced by the lasting effects of Locust Street on George Webber's self-identity: "It was a world which he had known and lived with every atom of his blood and brain and spirit, and every one of its thousand images was rooted in the structure of his life forever, as much a part of him as his inmost thoughts" (*WR*, 101). Similarly, to be "forever hillbound" (352) is, for Eugene Gant, to continue to view himself and the world through the window of a mountain-bred consciousness. Thus, it is a Wolfean axiom that not only can you not take the mountains out of the provincial, but you can also never wholly subtract the Locust Streets of childhood from the adult's psychic landscape. In an essay written for *The Asheville Citizen* (1937), Wolfe records how, when he "was far away" and "had been long from home" (*Return*, 1), he was still able to reconstruct in his mind, from the "ground" up, the inextricable landscapes of his hometown and childhood:

> Then all old things would come again—both brick and wall, and step and hedge, the way a street sloped or a tree was standing, the way a gate hung or a house was set, the very cinders of a rutted alley way—such things as these would come again, leaf, blade, and stone, and door. . . . all things like these would come again, the whole atomic pattern of my native earth, my town, my childhood and my youth . . . and all forgotten weathers of man's memory would come again, there in the darkness in some foreign land, would come so poignant, swift and vivid in the whiteness of their blazing panoply that I could feel . . . the whole sensuous unit of my native earth with an intensity that I had never known before. (1–2)

Similarly, in "No More Rivers," the Mississippi of George Hauser's childhood continues to exert a claim on his life and consciousness:

> That, he knew, had been *his* river. And for him, at least, it had been a good deal more than a river, a good deal more than an aspect of familiar geography. It was, in a way, the image of his whole life; his life had been haunted by that river; it had wound through the landscape of his youth like a haunted thread. In so many ways past knowing and past telling, he knew that this great stream—was his. (*CSS*, 610)

Implicit in these passages is Wolfe's acknowledgment—and celebration—that environments have recognizable topographical "personalities," especially those attached to "home." In "The Return of the Prodigal," Eugene Gant derives a compelling and poignant sense of "homing-in" from reading the familiar earth signs of the surrounding bioregion:

> Quickly, now, the hills drew in out of wide valleydom, and signs of old kept spaciousness vanished into the blue immediate. Here was another life, another language of its own—the life and language of creek, hill, and hollow, of gulch and notch and ridge and knob, and cabins nestling in their little patches of bottom land.

And suddenly Eugene was back in space and color and in time, the weather of his youth was round him, he was home again. (*HB,* 97)

Natural landscape cues are similarly used as homing devices in "His Father's Earth." Here, the story's young wanderer has a dream of returning to "his father's land," which he has never seen. As he surveys the land— "He saw the worn and ancient design of lichened rocks, the fertile soil of the baked fields, he saw the kept order, the frugal cleanliness, with its springtime growth, the mild tang of opulent greenery. There was an earth with fences" (*CSS,* 210–11)—the lineaments of its topography are strangely familiar ("like a room he once had lived in") because they "fit" his psychological map of what home should feel like: "Instantly he recognized the scene. He knew that he had come at last into his father's land. It was a magic that he knew but could not speak. . . . He knew every inch of the landscape, and he knew, past reason, doubt, or argument, that home was not three miles away" (211).

When Wolfe himself was abroad, his homesickness would become nationalized, stirring memories of various environmental phenomena which he associated with America: "it would be a bridge, the look of an old iron bridge across an American river, the sounds the train makes as it goes across it; the spoke-and-rumble of the ties below; the look of the muddy banks; the slow, thick, yellow wash of an American river" (*SN,* 32–33). As indicated by the "spoke and rumble" reference, impalpable phenomena are as integral a part of Wolfe's environmental landscapes as are tangible objects. Thus, a homesick and Europe-wandering Eugene Gant feels "home again" in America on the basis of aural cues alone, thinking "that he has heard there [in the night] the sounds of America and the wilderness" (*OTR,* 859):

And what are they? They are the whistle-wail of one of the great American engines as it thunders through the continent at night, the sound of the voices of the city streets—those hard, loud, slangy voices, full of violence, humor, and recklessness, now stronger and more remote than the sounds of Asia—the sounds that come up from the harbor of Manhattan at night—that magnificent orchestration of the transatlantics, the hoarse little tugs, the ferryboats and lighters, those sounds that well up from the gulf and dark immensity of night and that pierce the entrails of the listener. (859)

In Wolfe's texts, the presence of the environment is so ubiquitous that his landscapes of sight, sound, touch, and smell readily transcend the barriers between consciousness and the external world. The landscape is a force from within as well as from without.

Wolfe's environmental relationship was also informed by an acute sense of spatial consciousness, an orientation that is especially manifest in his "big picture" views of the landscape:

> Go seeker, if you will, throughout the land and you will find us [Americans] burning in the night.
>
> There where the hackles of the Rocky Mountains blaze in the blank and naked radiance of the moon, go make your resting stool upon the highest peak. Can you not see us now? The continental wall juts sheer and flat, its huge black shadow on the plain, and the plain sweeps out against the East, two thousand miles away. The great snake that you see there is the Mississippi River. (*YCGHA*, 391)

While this Olympian prospect of America's geography affords a suitable and epic stage from which Wolfe can deliver sage pronouncements on the character of America and Americans ("So, then, to every man his chance" [393]), it more importantly reflects Wolfe's aptitude for conceiving environments as situated within an expansive spatial continuum: from micro, to macro, to cosmic.

Wolfe, a man six-and-a-half feet tall, was always conscious of his spatial needs and circumstances, always seeking to escape the psychological crampedness of his physical surroundings, yet always mindful as well of both the beneficence and the terror of vast open spaces—the beneficence of their liberating vistas and the terror of their immensities "below the desolation of immense and cruel skies" (*OTR*, 412). These ambivalent sentiments, so characteristic of the man, are implicit in the following two letters (June 7 and July 3, 1938, respectively) that Wolfe wrote to Elizabeth Nowell during his western tour:

> What I saw of it [Idaho] today is the abomination of desolation: an enormous desert bounded by infinitely-far-away mountains that you never get to, and little pitiful blistered towns huddled down in the most abject loneliness underneath the huge light and scale and weather and the astonishing brightness and dimensions of everything—all given a kind of tremendousness and terror and majesty by the dimension. (*LTW*, 768)

this is a country fit for Gods—you've never seen anything like it for scale and magnificence and abundance: the trees are as tall as the Flatiron Building and yet so much in scale that you simply cannot believe, until you measure them, they are as big; and you throw a hook into some ordinary looking creek and pull out a twelve pound salmon. I assure you these things are literally true: you feel there's no limit, no end to anything. The East seems small and starved and meagre by comparison. (774–75)

Ambivalent or not, Wolfe viewed geographical America as sprawling in breadth: "He [Eugene Gant] brought back to it [the city] a tremendous memory of space, and power, and exultant distances" (*OTR*, 412). Hamilton Basso suggests that Wolfe's "preoccupation with space—with the bigness of America," "the huge illimitable earth of America" (*YCGHA*, 74)—was a kind of protest against the isolation in which he was vacuumed as a boy" (163), a symptomatic expression of "being forever hillbound." Maxwell Perkins similarly attributes Wolfe's expansive spatial vision, and especially his all-encompassing vision of America, to his hillbound childhood:

And so it was this ["imprisonment"] perhaps—and hearing the trains wind out around the labyrinthe mountains walls—that gave him his first great continental vision of America which was always his obsession. His imagination vaulted the mountains, and, fed by what he heard and read, and later saw, made him view the whole vast, sprawling, lonely land at once. ("Thomas Wolfe: A Writer for the People of His Time and Tomorrow," 3)

Wolfe's height further habituated him to apprehending his surroundings in terms of size, depth, and scale. Overall, then, he was predisposed—by his childhood environment, physical stature, and psychological orientation—to conceptualize both his personal condition and the "fit" of his environment from a spatial perspective. Thus, in the case of Thomas Wolfe and America, sweeping spatial vision met its complement in spatial sprawl ("He needed a continent to range over, actually and in imagination. And his place was all America" [Perkins, "Thomas Wolfe," *LHA*, xiv]) and, as illustrated in the scene in *You Can't Go Home Again* where the narrator describes the crowd at the Admiral Drake Hotel looking up to where C. Green has just fallen to his death, Wolfean optics met its complement in American optics:

Their eyes go traveling upward slowly—up—up—up. The building seems to widen curiously, to be distorted, to flare out wedgelike til it threatens to annihilate the sky, overwhelm the will, and crush the spirit. (These optics, too, American, Admiral Drake). (368)

In fact, Wolfe's spatial consciousness may be viewed as his own variation on a quintessentially native outlook, one which is drawn to wide open spaces and bigness in scale. Charles Olson invokes this American-bred spatial optics when he asserts, "I take SPACE to be the central fact to man born in America, from Folsom cave to now. I spell it large because it comes large. Large, and without mercy" (*Call Me Ishmael,* 11). Wolfe's sublime description of the "tremendousness and terror and majesty" of Idaho embodies Olson's credo, and his literary approach to space demonstrates the extent to which Wolfe's psychological orientation to the landscape merges with a foundational American perspective.

Ultimately, Wolfe could not fully conceive the contours and reality of his narrative world—including his conceptions of the self, human character, humanity, home, place, Americans, America, and life itself—without reference to the *natural* world. Thus, human character in a Wolfe novel is not merely shaped by environmental forces, but ultimately rooted in nature. And, as we shall see, nature's presence is everywhere in Wolfe's texts—even in, under, and around the hard pavements and inorganic mazes of urban habitats. Being "everywhere," nature is also the dimension which gives coherence and integrity to both his fictional dramas and his vision of life.

Chapter Three

Nature

Touchstone, Source, and Kin

While Thomas Wolfe grew up and moved away from his hometown of Asheville, he never outgrew the mountain-locked, green expanse of western North Carolina. In fact, the processes of the natural world surrounding Asheville became for him a universal analogue, influencing his language, thinking, and outlook for the remainder of his life. As a result, his treatment of nature in his texts exposes his values and beliefs about not only the natural world, but the human world as well. In fact, his texts suggest that he came to conceive both worlds as interrelated.

The milieu that first wakened Wolfe's consciousness to nature was not the overarching setting of the mountains, but the more modest setting of his first home and its surrounding lot at 92 Woodfin Street. Here, the lush vegetation of the property and the viny, embowered mantle of the house framed the first six years of his life.[1] In her reminiscences of her childhood, Mabel Wheaton, one of Wolfe's sisters, describes a pastoral idyll, "a profusion of flowers, fruit trees, and flowering shrubs" (17). Wolfe's father, Oliver, had built this house for his former wife, Cynthia, and was primarily responsible for superintending the trees, vegetables, fruits, and flowers on the property. It was also Oliver Wolfe who first introduced his son Thomas to the enchantments of the outdoors:

> One day the next spring when Tom was seven months old, Papa took him out under the trees in the backyard. All the world seemed in blossom; the yard was a mass of blooms and the trees and shrubs harbored many birds. Papa wanted Tom to see and smell the flowers and hear the birds sing. (Wheaton, *Thomas Wolfe and His Family*, 47).

Wolfe memorializes this landmark day in *Look Homeward, Angel:*

> One day when the opulent Southern Spring had richly unfolded, when the spongy black earth of the yard was covered with sudden, tender grass, and wet blossoms, the great cherry tree seethed slowly with a massive

gem of amber sap, and the cherries hung ripening in prodigal clusters, Gant took him from his basket in the sun on the high front porch, and went with him around the house by the lily bed, taking him back under the trees singing with hidden birds, to the far end of the lot. (32)

Years later, Wolfe continued to associate his childhood with Woodfin Street's immediate green surroundings, as evidenced by the following letter he wrote to his mother Julia in late May, 1923, when he was twenty-two:

When Spring comes I think of a cool, narrow back yard in North Caro-lina with green, damp earth, and cherry trees in blossom. I think of a skinny little boy at the top of one of those trees, with the fragrant blooms about him, with the tang of the sap in his nose, looking out on a world of back yards, and building Castles in Spain. (*LTM*, 43)

Julia Wolfe's own interest in nature was a legacy of her childhood, having been, like the Eliza Gant of *Of Time and the River*, "born and brought up in the country—close to the lap of Mother Earth, as the sayin' goes" (241). She tended her own vegetable garden, canned fruits and vegetables, and made wine and strawberry jam. Both parents loved flowers.

Beyond the confined setting of Woodfin Street was, of course, the circle of mountains: "From Woodfin Street, as from every part of Asheville, the great mountains are visible. Almost every street ends in a vista of moun-tains" (Adams, *Thomas Wolfe, Carolina Student: A Brief Biography*, 10). As a result, the children's interest in the earth inevitably extended to the nature-rich countryside: "Thousands of streams and waterfalls lace the forests with the 'rock bright flowing water' which Tom Wolfe loved. . . . 'Tell me if the wonderful mountain Spring has come yet,' Wolfe wrote his mother from New York" (10–11).

Wolfe's relationship with nature was also influenced by his initial expo-sure to the regional landscapes of the South and, in the case of the family's trip to St. Louis, parts of the Midwest. Julia Wolfe took trips into the South to ease her rheumatism during the winters; stops included New Orleans, St. Petersburg, Tampa, Palm Beach, Jacksonville, St. Augustine, Daytona, Hot Springs, Knoxville, and Washington, D.C. Judging by Wolfe's handling of Eugene Gant's perceptions and sentiments, Wolfe's first impressions of these landscapes beyond his familiar rim of hills were significant and last-ing. It is likely, for instance, that his romance with rivers, which originally centered on the Mississippi, began about this time. In recounting the trip to St. Louis in *Look Homeward, Angel,* Wolfe describes how "Eugene watched the sun wane and redden on a rocky river, and on the painted rocks of Tennessee gorges: the enchanted river wound into his child's mind forever. Years later, it was to be remembered in dreams tenanted with elvish and mysterious beauty" (44). Similarly, in *Of Time and the River,* Starwick speaks of his childhood-born attachment to "the great slow river—the dark and secret river of the night—the everlasting flood—the unceasing Mississippi. It is a river I know so well, with all my life that I shall never tell about" (324).

Wolfe's romance with the sea was probably initiated on the same childhood trips into the South and, as is the case with Wolfe's rivers, it also figures prominently throughout his writings. In *Look Homeward, Angel,* "hill-bound" Eugene Gant greets the Atlantic at Daytona as the wondrous realization of his sea fantasies; finally, he is able to see "the long seaplunges in the unending scroll-work of the emerald and infinite sea, which had beat in his brain from his father's shells, which had played at his mountain heart, but which never, until now, had he seen" (133). Later, in college, Eugene's shell-haunted enchantment is reawakened during his Greek studies by "the vast sea-surge of Homer" (*LHA,* 334).

Thus, the close proximity of nature in his backyard and in the surrounding landscape, his travels through the South, and his parents' valuation of the earth, its procreative powers, and the beauty of its flora encouraged young Thomas Wolfe to look upon the nonhuman world with interest, appreciation, and curiosity. Given also his aesthetic consciousness and hyper-sensual orientation to the world, Wolfe subsequently developed a naturalist's eye for observing the phenomena of nature; he became an inveterate watcher of the earth, the sky, the sea, the weather, and the seasons. More to the point, Wolfe's observations of nature became incorporated into his writings as he grew to view the natural world as playing an integral role in human existence. In fact, his story-making itself became reliant on his use of nature and, as a result, his many images of, and references to, the nonhuman world seem to grow organically around the lives and events of his protagonists. It is also telling that while he continued to observe and fictionalize his observations of nature throughout his life, his earliest memories have especially had enormous staying power in his writings. It is as if his first memories of the earth were epiphanies that he needed to play over and over again, sifting for new meanings. Just as his first experiences with rivers continued to reverberate throughout his texts, so his childhood fascination with mountains inaugurated an ongoing dialogue with mountain imagery and associations.[2] Similarly, the wild winds that played around the eaves of his childhood home in Asheville continued to play throughout not only the pages of his novels, but his life as well. In the following letter to Aline Bernstein (Nov. 10, 1926), he writes:

> It is a grey fierce morning: the wind is howling against the trees. I have been standing at my window watching the dead leaves which fill the air in flocks, and the trees growing visibly bare before my eyes, and the blown rain spits against my window. I have in my heart the wild exalting the wind and the rain always bring, and a nameless terror. (*MOL*, 118)

Smitten by his first exposures to the natural landscapes of his childhood, Wolfe was haunted by his originary images of them throughout his life. "Thus did he see first," Wolfe writes, "he the hill-bound, the sky-girt, of whom the mountains were his masters, the fabulous South. The picture of flashing field, of wood, and hill, stayed in his heart forever" (*LHA*, 133).

Wolfe's references to "the earth" are so pervasive and frequent, especially in *Look Homeward Angel* and *Of Time and the River*, that they resemble an ongoing incantation: "The enormous earth resumed its silence" (*FDTM*, 194), "All that we know is that the earth is flowing by us in the darkness" (*OTR*, 34), "Spring was coming on again across the earth" (*LHA*, 423), "The earth was ours because we loved the earth" (*WR*, 632), "His was the voice, the tongue, the language of everyone of these who had lived and died and gone unrecorded to the earth" (*HB*, 164), "All things belonging to the earth will never change" (*YCGHA*, 40). Although Wolfe's concept of the nonhuman world also encompassed the sea and the sky, the earth was his anchor in the cosmos and his universal metaphor for "nature."

The earth is also immortal, and its immortality is both disquieting and reassuring. On the one hand, its timelessness serves to assuage and suspend the anxieties of a world in flux. Thus, when George Webber returns to his hometown of Libya Hill, he is reassured by the unchanging presence of the hills: "When he looked from the windows of the train next morning the hills were there . . . and it seemed to him that he had never left the hills, and all that had passed in the years between was like a dream"

(*YCGHA*, 75). Similarly, Eugene and Laura find solace in their "timeless valley," cached away in the same hills: "'What time is it?' Eugene asked. For they had come to a place where no time was" (*LHA*, 378). Wolfe himself experienced this timelessness of nature when, on his return visit to Asheville in 1937, he noted how the town—but especially the encircling hills—had remained unchanged. In the presence of a local newsperson, Wolfe reportedly lifted his eyes to the rim of hills that surrounded the city "and said to the somewhat startled reporter, 'You can't change the mountains'" (Donald, *Look Homeward*, 415).[3] Nature's timelessness—what Wolfe coined "time immutable, the time of rivers, mountains, oceans, and the earth" (*SN*, 52)—is also an implacable presence "against which [is] projected the transience of man's life, the bitter briefness of his day" (52), and this capacity of the earth to confront humanity with its own mortality is poignantly chronicled in the following passage, where Boston-bound Eugene Gant and his friends meditate on the Virginia landscape as it unfolds past their train window:

> The earth emerged with all its ancient and eternal quality: stately and solemn and lonely-looking in that first light, it filled men's hearts with all its ancient wonder. It seemed to have been there forever. . . . They knew that they would die and that the earth would last forever. (*OTR*, 76–77)[4]

This "eternal quality" of nature was also conflated, for Wolfe, with reality, truth, and integrity. Thus, the Boston-bound youths "felt nothing but silence and wonder in their hearts, and were naked and alone and stripped down to their bare selves, as near to truth as men can ever become" (77). Feeling humbled in the earth's presence, they act as if they are returning the gaze of a righteous god. In *Look Homeward, Angel*, Eugene is comforted by the "honesty" of the ocean's sounds juxtaposed to the carnival's noisy flimflammery at his back: "But the only sound that was real, that was near and present, was the sound in his heart, in his brain, of the everlasting sea. He turned his face toward it: behind him, the cheap million lights of the concessionaires, the clatter, the racket" (436). Similarly, when Eugene first comes to New York City and feels paranoically surrounded by "foul mistrust and lying slander" (*OTR*, 421), he finds consolation in the tangible true-ness of nature's enduring existence, its infrangible is-ness. Thus, after he recounts to himself "the incredible magic of the peach bloom in the month of April, the smell of rivers after rain" (422), and other eternal rites of nature, he feels reassured that "these facts . . . [are] as literal as nails to fix the hides of falsehood to the wall, as real as April and all magic whatsoever" (422). We are also told that George Webber's goat-cries are so very "right" because "the cry had welled up from the earth with a relentless certitude, and all the gold and glory of the earth was in it. It had been for him a touchstone to reality, for it had never played him false" (WR, 564).

The essence of human existence was, for Wolfe, not only measured against the "changeless change" (OTR, 245) of the nonhuman world, but against its vastness as well; the earth's immensity confronts humans with their relative smallness in the cosmos. Thus, Wolfe notes of the Boston-bound youths, "So here they are now, three atoms on the huge breast of the indifferent earth, three youths out of a little town walled far away within the great rim of the silent mountains, already a distant, lonely dot upon the immense and sleeping visage of the continent" (OTR, 68). This overview of nature and humanity is overwhelmingly ecocentric and, in fact, Wolfe viewed human existence as a tragic and heroic struggle to make a place for itself in a vast, indifferent universe.[5]

It is important to keep in mind, however, that when Wolfe contemplated "the earth," he usually meant the *American* earth: "For only the earth endures, but this earth is America, and America is this earth, and while this earth endures, America endures. America is immense and ever-lasting" (A, 46). For Wolfe, America was not only conflated with the earth, but defined by it as well; it is ultimately the sum of its weather, seasons, skies, earth, rivers, lakes, and mountains. It is, says Wolfe, "the place of the howling winds, the hurrying of the leaves in old October, the hard clean falling to the earth of acorns" (OTR, 155). Accordingly, the "real history" of Old Catawba (Wolfe's fictionalized North Carolina) is the history of the relationship between Old Catawbans and their state's natural environment:

> The real history of Old Catawba is not essentially a history of wars or rebellions; it is not a history of democracy or plutocracy or any form of government. . . . The real history of Old Catawba is a history of solitude, of the wilderness, and of the eternal earth, it is the history of millions of men living and dying alone in the wilderness, it is the history of the billion unrecorded and forgotten acts and moments of their lives; it is a

history of the sun and the moon and the earth, of the sea that feathers eternally against the desolate coasts, and of great trees that smash down in lone solitudes of the wilderness. ("The Men of Old Catawba," *FDTM*, 203–4)[6]

Not only does nature characterize America's states, but it also binds them together:

Meanwhile the Palisades are melting in massed molten colors, the season swings along the nation, and a little later in the South dense woodings on the hill begin to glow and soften, and when they smell the burning wood-smoke in Ohio children say: "I'll bet that there's a forest fire in Michigan". . . . Meanwhile the leaves are turning, turning, up in Maine, the chestnut burrs plop thickly to the earth in gusts of wind, and in Virginia the chinkapins are falling. (*OTR*, 330)

The extent of Wolfe's valuation of, and affinity for, America's natural environment is made clear in a letter to Maxwell Perkins (July 1, 1930) in which he compares his environmental stance toward America with Fitzgerald's: "we had quite an argument about America: I said we were a homesick people, and belonged to the earth and land we came from as much or more as any country I knew about—he said we were not, that we were not a country, that he had no feeling for the land he came from" (*LTW*, 237–38).

Fitzgerald notwithstanding, Wolfe conceptualized Americans as not only attached to their land, but also imbued with its "wild" and spacious character, "the savage, unfenced, and illimitable wilderness of the country" (*FDTM*, 111). "Our senses," writes Wolfe, "have been fed by our terrific land" (*LHA*, 352). America is "the place of the storm-tossed moanings of the wintry mountainside, where the young men cry out in their throats and feel the savage vigor, the rude strong energies" (*OTR*, 155). Moreover, the wildness of the American earth distinguishes it from the natural landscapes of other countries. By comparison, France's landscape is too civilized: "It did not look like America: the land looked fat and well kept, and even the smoky wintry woods had this well-kept appearance" (*OTR*, 797). The natural scene is also bigger in America than anywhere else: "We walked along a road in Cumberland [England], and stooped, because the sky hung down so low; and when we ran away from London, we went by little rivers in a land just big enough. And nowhere that we went was far: the earth and the sky were close and near" (*LHA*, 352). Even the seasons are different in America: "Now October has come again which in our land is different from October in the other lands" (*OTR*, 329).

Wolfe's love of American nature is not only broadcast in his writings, but also evident in comments he made to others. While surveying the Mississippi during a visit to New Orleans, "Wolfe picked up a tuft of grass, held it high, and watched as the wind blew it away from his open palm. 'This, fellows, this is America,' he boomed, 'and that river is some river'" (Magi and Walser, *Thomas Wolfe Interviewed: 1929–1938*, 73). A similar testimonial may be read in Wolfe's comments on a rural train station, which he visited at night in the company of his sister Mabel and a friend, Kathleen Hoagland. With patriotic fervor, Wolfe treats this human artifact as an organic part of a vast and nationalized ecosystem where everything from insects to the moon is "made in America":

> "This is America! All over the country there are little stations like this one, with a tree. . . . "Come along," he said. "I want to show you how you should write. See these walls? Feel them. Look at that color. They are yellow; they are faded yellow. . . . Feel the ground," he said. "Put your hands on the ground." He said, "Listen to the insects. Look! The moon is shining over all this eastern part of America. This is America. This is America, Kitty." (Wheaton, 325)

In Wolfe's cosmic overview, the sky—"the immense and timeless skies that bend above us" (*OTR*, 209)—and the sea—"the limitless . . . desert of the sea" (282), "the timeless, yearless sea" (*WR*, 285)—are also vast and immortal. However, although they can be experienced affirmatively—the sea "like a woman lying below [herself] on the coral floor" (*LHA*, 436), and the sky as "pearl light" (149)—both remain, despite their moments of beauty, alien and remote presences for humankind.[7] By contrast, Wolfe does not portray the earth as an alien presence; rather, it is experienced as kin to humankind, a nurturant force which is, at the same time, indifferent to who or what seeks its succor; thus, he refers to "the huge breast of the indifferent earth." "The earth," writes Wolfe, "is our mother and our nurse, and we can know her" (*FDTM*, 187); it is "the fixed principle, *the female principle*" (*LTW*, 235). Wolfe acknowledges this nurturant quality by negation when commenting on "the whole earth-detachment of the sea" (*OTR*, 856), the truth of which is dramatically illustrated by the experience of George Webber and his fellow passengers on the ship, *Vesuvia,* as it rides out a storm en route to America:

> Then, for the first time, many people lying in that ship's dark hull felt the power and the terror of the sea. . . . It comes but once to the sons of earth, but wherever it comes, though they be buried in some ship's dark hold, they know that they have met the sea. For it is everything that the earth is not, and in that moment men know the earth as their mother and friend. (*WR,* 282)

At the same time, storm-wracked ships embody their own salvation by having been made from the same earth: "Their terror of the ocean was touched with pride and joy—this ship, smelted from the enduring earth, this ship, wrought and riveted from the everlasting land, this ship . . . would bring them through the awful seas to safety on strange shores."

While the human life span is infinitely brief compared to the millennia of rivers, mountains, and oceans, Wolfe emphasized that human life is as much a part of the organic world as nonhuman life; that humans and mountains are, in fact, related. Thus, Wolfe often made allusions to "the great family of the earth to which all men belong" (*OTR,* 755). The earth is also the origin, home, and clay of humankind. In fact, Wolfe's texts suggest that not only can we "go home again" to the earth when we die, but that, as kin to the earth, we are always already home, our very substance derived from the nonhuman world all around us. Thus, Wolfe refers to "the everlasting earth, from which we have been derived, wherein again we shall be compacted" (246). In "Gulliver," Wolfe explains the tall protagonist's commonality with all people with the simple observation, "For he is earthy, of the earth, like every man" (*FDTM,* 137). "We are," notes Coker in *Look Homeward, Angel,* "a flash of fire—a brain, a heart, a spirit. And we are three-cents-worth of lime and iron—which we cannot get back" (461). In addressing this elemental affinity between humans and the earth, Wolfe especially liked to invoke the lives of the American pioneers. He was proud of his own pioneer ancestry and valued the fact that early Americans had been more a part of nature by having lived with fewer barriers between themselves and the elements; they had, Wolfe relates, "sowed their blood and sperm across the continent, walked beneath its broad and lonely lights, were frozen by its bitter cold, burned by the heat of its fierce suns" (*OTR,* 413).

In being compacted of the earth, humans also share a kinship with all organic life. Thus, George Webber refers to himself as "Time's plant" (*YCGHA*, 572), and Wolfe treats the retrieval of George's memories as an organic movement "back" to the originary root fibers of his existence: "so did the plant [of memory] go back, stem by stem, root by root, and filament by filament, until it was complete and whole, compacted of the very earth that had produced it, and of which it was itself the last and living part" (573–74). Wolfe also viewed human beings ("Man") as part animals—"this frail and petty thing who lives his day and dies like all the other animals" (339–40)—and, accordingly, he dramatizes the latent feral consciousness of his protagonists. Thus, Eugene suddenly feels his animal self emerge as he surveys Altamont from a hill above it: "It seemed to him suddenly that he had not come up on the hill from the town, but that he had come out of the wilderness like a beast, and was staring now with steady beast-eye at this huddle of wood and mortar" (*LHA*, 375). Wolfe's use of animal references, images, and similes in characterizations serves not only to expose the buried animal nature of human beings, but also to illuminate various nuances of human character that might otherwise be overlooked: "old men and women from the country on first visits to their children in the city . . . looked about them constantly and suspiciously with the quick eyes of birds and animals, alert, mistrustful, and afraid" (*YCGHA*, 45). As earth dwellers, humans not only have a kinship with flora and fauna, but are also caught in the same ecological web as is all nonhuman life: "not a sparrow fell through the air but that its repercussion acted on [Eugene's] life, and the lonely light that fell upon the viscous and interminable seas at dawn awoke sea-changes washing life to him" (*LHA*, 160).

Being part animals, humans are equipped with sensory capacities which are fundamentally primal in nature, and Wolfe believed that humans could best nourish themselves by using these capacities to tap nature's energies; thus, human vitality could be drawn from sensory contact with mountains, skies, and winds. As evidence of this energetic infusion, young George Webber feels windswept inside as he inhales the life-affirming drafts of a mountain wind: "And that wind would rush upon him with its own wild life and fill him with its spirit . . . his whole life seemed to soar, to swoop, to yell with the demonic power, flight, and invincible caprice of the wind's huge well" (*WR*, 152). This vitalization process is also dramatized when Eugene Gant, being quickened by the life-stirring processes of spring, is temporarily overcome by his animal nature:

> He hurtled down the campus lanes, bounding along like a kangaroo, leaping high at the lower branches to clip a budding twig with his teeth. He cried loudly in his throat—a whinnying squeal—the centaur-cry of man or beast, trying to unburden its overladed heart in one blast of pain and joy and passion. (*LHA*, 348)

George Webber is possessed at times by the same animalistic persona. His "wild goat-cry of pain and joy and ecstasy" (559) is his vital and elemental response to life, and, as in Eugene's case, it is especially evoked by the illimitable range of nature's forms: "Sometimes the cry was packed into the passing of a cloud upon the massed green of a hill, and sometimes, with the most intolerable ecstasy that he had ever known, it was in the green light of the woods, the lyric tangle of the wilderness, the cool, bare spaces underneath a canopy of trees" (*WR*, 560).[8] Again and again throughout Wolfe's oeuvre, his characters are stimulated and enlivened by their contact with the nonhuman world.

Wolfe himself was similarly energized. When Robert Raynolds went sledding with his wife and Wolfe one night, he found Wolfe shouting on a hill with his own animalistic ardor:

> I saw Tom's big sled in the snow at the foot of the hill but I did not see him. Then I heard him yell at the night, and saw him on the mounded edge of our little sand pit, down near the school house where I wrote my novels. His back was to me. He was tossing his arms and yelping with loud animal vigor. He was like a dark giant at primitive rejoicing in the fields of snow. (117)

Accordingly, Wolfe's protagonists favor "wild" nature over its "cultivated" forms. Thus, Wolfe's ironic treatment of the city dweller, Mr. Jack, and his "country baron" approach to the green world: "Although city-bred, Mr. Jack was as sensitive to the charms of Mother Earth as any man alive. He liked the cultivated forms of nature—the swarded lawns of great estates, gay regiments of brilliant garden flowers, and rich masses of clumped shrubbery" (*YCGHA*, 125). Even when we are told that Mr. Jack "also liked the ruder and more natural forms of *beauty*" [emphasis mine]—such as when, during a trip into the country, he was "touched by the cosmic

sadness of leafy orange, gold, and russet brown in mid-October" (126)—
Wolfe implies that his response remains aesthetic rather than elemental.
After all, Wolfe's narrator observes drily, "Mr. Jack always came back to the
city. For life was real, and life was earnest, and Mr. Jack was a business
man" (126). The implication is that, for the likes of Mr. Jack, nature is a
timeout from the "real" world. For Wolfe, of course, nature is the ultimate
measure of what is real.

In his fiction, Wolfe does more than chronicle the human capacity
to maintain contact with nature and one's own primal self; he celebrates
it. Just as he speaks affirmatively of Eugene Gant's and George Webber's
animal-cries, so he valorizes the strong bonds with the earth shared by
Gant and the Eliza character in the novella, "The Web of Earth." Gant, he
of the "earth-devouring stride" (*OTR,* 241), is figured as being able to
impregnate the soil with his own elemental vitality, the earth responding
with teeming plant life: "wherever his great hands touched the earth it
grew fruitful for him" (*LHA,* 14); "The earth was spermy for him like a big
woman" (55); and "The earth receives my seed. For me the great lettuces.
Spongy and full of sap now like a woman. The thick grapevine—in August
the heavy clustered grapes—How there? Like milk from a breast" (150–51).
In using sexual imagery to figure Gant's relationship to the procreative
powers of the earth, Wolfe implies that sensual contact between humans
and nature can be as intense and intimate as sexual union.

If Wolfe figures Gant as both a conduit and an amorous partner of
nature, he portrays the Eliza character in "The Web of Earth" as earth-wise
and rooted in the rhythms of the seasons.⁹ In recalling the past events of
her life while visiting her son, Eugene, in New York City, she confesses, "I
reckon for a fact I had the power of Nature in me" (*FDTM,* 297), adding,
"Why, yes! . . . couldn't I make things grow by touchin' them, and wasn't
it that way ever since I was a child—termaters and flowers and corn and
vegetables—and all kinds of fruit" (300). In bruiting her ability to conjure
food from the earth, she also predicts, "If the worst comes to the worst, I
wouldn't starve, if I didn't have a penny I could live, I'd make the earth
produce for me. I've done it and I could do it yet" (300). She further notes,
sententiously, "We've always got the earth. We'll stand upon it and it will
save us. It's never gone back on nobody yet" (303). At the end of "The
Web of Earth," Eliza feels drawn back to the South to experience the

efflorescence of spring in her backyard. Feeling the familial tug of her southern earth, she reminds her son of his own roots:

> Now it will soon be April, and I must be going home again: out in my garden where I work, the early flowers and blossoms will be comin' out, the peach trees and the cherry trees, the dogwood and the laurel and the lilacs. I have an apple tree and it is full of all the birds there are in June: the flower-tree you planted as a child is blooming by the window where you planted it. . . . The hills are beautiful and soon it will be spring once more. (It worries me to think of you like this, alone and far away: child, child, come home again!). (304)[10]

While Wolfe believed that people can reveal themselves through their ecological contact with any and all surroundings, he viewed the organic world, being an extension of ourselves, as especially constituted to draw out the defining elements of a person's character. Thus, the characters of Gant and Eliza are cast in relief as they interact with the natural world, and, similarly, it is through Eugene's and George's contact with nature that we are able to see the full play of their perceptiveness, sensitivity, emotionality, and sensual and aesthetic awareness. Such nature-based characterizations also reflect the depth and scope of Wolfe's own nature consciousness. Young George Webber, for example, evinces not only an acute awareness of, and communion with, the natural world, but a self-satisfied knowingness about it as well:

> George lay in the grass and pulled some grass blades and looked upon them contentedly and chewed upon them. And he knew the way the grass blades were. He dug bare toes into the grass and thought of it. He knew the way it felt. Among the green grass, he saw patches of old brown, and he knew the way that was too. He put out his hand and felt the maple tree. He saw the way it came out of the earth, the grass grew right around it, he felt the bark and got its rough, coarse feeling. He pressed hard with his fingers, a little rough piece of bark came off: he knew the way that was too. The wind kept howling faintly the way it does in May. All the young leaves of the maple tree turned back, straining in the wind. He heard the sound it made, it touched him with sadness, then the wind went and came again. (*WR*, 24)

George is portrayed as someone who intuitively knows how nature works and what it is, suggesting that, for Wolfe, we already "know" nature, at some elemental level, as we know our kin. George's interactions also suggest the deep level of interpenetration that is possible between humans and nature. Whereas his innate knowingness is able to penetrate the mask of nature, nature, on its part, is able to penetrate his body and draw out his feelings; thus, the wind's sound "touched him [George] with sadness." Such close affinity with nature is also evident in Eugene's recognition of autumn's sounds and emotional resonance in *Look Homeward, Angel:* "The streets at night were filled with sad lispings: all through the night, upon his porch, as in a coma, he heard the strange noise of autumn" (396).

While Wolfe celebrated the capacity of human beings for communion with nature, he also exposed their equal and more characteristic capacity for becoming alienated from it. This separation process is, for Wolfe, especially endemic to those who inhabit urban environments, and he draws considerable attention in his fiction to what happens when city dwellers are deprived of regular contact with the earth: they became devitalized, detached from both the green world "outside" and their own animal natures. Wolfe analogizes city people to plants that lack sufficient water and nutrients; they become parched, "as if their ten thousand days and nights upon the rootless pavement had dried all juice and succulence out of them, as if asphalt and brick and steel had got into the conduits of their blood and spirit" (*OTR*, 457–58). The constructed environment serves to obscure any earth signs from even the most alert senses: "they [city youth] rarely knew the feel of earth beneath their feet and no birds sang, their youthful eyes grew hard, unseeing, from being stopped forever by a wall of masonry" (*YCGHA*, 333). In alluding to the opening of *Moby Dick* (1851), where Melville "tells how the city people of his time would, on every occasion that was afforded them, go down to the dock . . . and stand there looking out to sea" (333), Wolfe suggests that contemporary urbanites harbor the same innate, nature-seeking desire, but that "in the great city of today, . . . there is no sea to look out to, or if there is, it is so far away, so inaccessible, walled in behind such infinite ramifications of stone and steel, that the effort to get to it is disheartening" (333). To compensate for their diminished contact with the natural life-giving energies of the green world, urbanites draw on the artificial energy of the city's frantic pace, "as if they . . . could keep going only by a kind of lifeless dynamism, a dry electric energy which paced them to the tempo of the city's furious life" (*OTR*, 504). Eugene Gant sees the debilitating effects of this contra-green climate on the Murphys, an Irish family that has become "deracinated" from its country-bred heritage:

> There was nothing warm, rich, or generous about them or their lives: it seemed as if the living roots of nature had grown gnarled and barren among the walls and pavements of the city, it seemed that everything that is wild, sudden, capricious, whimsical, passionate, and mysterious in the spirit of the [Irish] race had been dried and hardened out of them by their divorce from the magical earth their fathers came from, as if the snarl and jangle of the city streets, the barren and earthless angularity of steel and stone and brick, had entered their souls. (161)

Conversely, Webber views the hill-born Irish from his hometown as more fully human and alive because they live closer to the earth and, as a result, have thrived: "it seemed to him that they belonged to a grander and completely different race; or perhaps, he thought, the glory of earth and air and sky there had kept them ripe and sweet as they always were, while their brothers here had withered upon the rootless pavements" (166). It is not so much that city denizens are shaped by brick, but that they are *not* shaped by the natural world; it is environmental conditioning by default. As a result, even consciousness of the earth can become paved over. Thus, in wondering about the relationship between New York City–bred Abe Jones and the nonhuman world, Wolfe addresses the plight of all city dwellers when he asks,

> What earth had nourished him? Had he been born and grown there among the asphalt lilies and pavement wheat? What corn was growing from the cobblestones? Or was there never a cry of earth up through the beaten and unyielding cement of the streets? Had he forgotten the immortal and attentive earth still waiting at the roots of steel? (458)

In "No More Rivers," Wolfe tells the tragic story of a city dweller who *wants* to escape nature's presence. The protagonist, George Hauser, is a person who has migrated from the country and now seeks to withdraw from life. Although he is fascinated by the welter of teeming life that he sees borne on the river that flows past his harborside apartment, he ultimately feels assaulted and agitated by the "the living energy of all [the river's] veined and weaving currents, the constant traffics of its multiform and never-ending life—with all their evocations of the violence of living" (CSS, 603). As a result, he recoils from the river's raucous vitality—in the same way as T. S. Eliot's narrator recoils from the vibrancy of spring in "The Waste Land"—and, by the end of the story, ends up blocking "that shining river of life" (611) from sight altogether by closing his venetian blinds. "Now," writes Wolfe, "there were no more rivers" (611). As a result, George Hauser, who has become increasingly more hermitic, now fully embraces a nature-impoverished half-life. In what amounts to a parable, Wolfe suggests that any existence apart from the *living* rivers of life, the stream of nature, is unnatural and deadening to the spirit.[11]

Despite the stultifying effects of the urban landscape, Wolfe acknowledges that there are certain exceptional people who are able not only to survive, but actually to thrive, in the city environs. In portraying Esther Jack as one of these people, he describes a woman who draws both her robustness ("her apple cheeks would glow with health and freshness" [YCGHA, 133]) and her energy ("She seemed to be charged with all the good and joyful living of the earth" [WR, 410]) from the organic vitality of nature; and, in fact, she resembles a city plant that *is* flourishing: "She was the natural growth of steel, stone, and masonry, yet she was as fresh, juicy, and rosy as if she had come out of the earth" (352). As a result, when she mingles with the sidewalk traffic, she appears to be an anomaly, a well-spring amid a human desert:

> when she went out on the streets, among the thrusting throngs of deso-late and sterile people, her face shone forth like a deathless flower among their dead, grey flesh and dark, dead eyes. . . . Her whole figure with its fertile curves, opulent as the earth, belonged to an order of humanity so different from that of their own starved barrenness. (YCGHA, 133)

While city dwellers are especially disadvantaged in terms of being cut off from the earth, Wolfe suggests, that no matter where people live, the prevailing conditions of our modern culture militate against meaningful contact with the earth. As a result, "from his cradle to his grave ["man"] scarcely sees the sun or moon or stars; he is unconscious of the immortal sea and earth" (337).

Wolfe himself, however, *was* able to "see green" in urban spaces, and it was this salvaged green that constituted most of the buried light he uncovered in America's cities. While we can to some extent attribute nature's presence in his fictional cities to his "initial view of the world [being] broadly characteristic of the nineteenth-century organic and evolutionary mode of thinking" (Boyle, "Thomas Wolfe: Theme through Imagery," 263); to a concerted effort by Wolfe to participate in what James L. Machor calls the "rural-urban synthesis," that is, "the resulting dialogue between the culture and its artists over the viability of fusing the city and the garden" (23); and to a process of familiarization by a stranger in a strange land; in fact, the presence of nature in Wolfe's city-based narratives attests primarily to his nature-tuned senses and the green world's ever-present hold on his consciousness. It *is* true that Wolfe, a writer from the provinces, first saw the city through country spectacles and, therefore, to some extent initially *imposed* his organic tropes as well as his mythical vision of the city as a frontier or wilderness.[12] In fact, A. Carl Bredahl Jr. points out that the use of familiar language and locutions to "enclose" alien territory has been a prominent aspect of American literature. "Over and over," asserts Bredahl, "American narrators are torn between their desire to trust the language that defines the new world as an Eden or a City on a Hill and their recognition that the enclosures of culture and language conflict with the experience of life in America" (*New Ground*, 27). While it may be true that Wolfe himself initially tried to "tame" the city with his green rhetoric and then began to move toward more objective representations, at no time does his treatment of the city suggest that he ever lost sight of nature's actual presence in and around the city environs. If Wolfe came to figure the city less frequently in organic terms, he never let go of his notion, and never ceased suggesting in his texts, that the city *inhabits* an organic world.

Wolfe, himself a city dweller, made efforts throughout his life to maintain contact with nature. On a trip with Raynolds through Vermont, Wolfe climbed hills, washed his feet in streams, visited a marble quarry, hiked through woods, and walked down country roads. Wolfe's appreciative, even beatific, response to the outdoors is indicated by Raynolds' sketch of him surveying a panorama of mountains: "There was a ruddy flush on his face. His brows were relaxed. His eyes, full of a thousand gorgeous playings of light from the valley and the ranges, were steady, steadfast, and luminous. . . . There he stood . . . gazing about the world in radiant poise of quiet joy" (94). In commenting on this trip in a letter to his mother (Sept.

13, 1933), Wolfe plays up the salubrious effects of being able to escape the city's turbulent environment and recharge himself: "I feel better than I have felt in months. It is such a relief to get away from all the confusion, noise, and fatigue of the city into all this peace and beauty" (*LTM*, 212). In his fiction, Wolfe treats the passage from the city to the country as not only an energizing process, but a purgative one as well:

> As he [George Webber] felt the abiding strength and everlastingness of the earth, he began to feel also a sense of exultation and release. . . . He that has known only a jungle of mortared brick and stone where no birds sing, where no blade grows, has now found earth again. And yet, unfathomable enigma that it is, he has found earth and, finding it, has lost the world. He has found the washed cleanliness of vision and of soul that comes from earth. He feels himself washed free of all stains of ancient living, its evil and its lust, its filth and cruelty, its perverse and ineradicable pollution. (*YCGHA*, 453)

In an effort to salve his own fevered spirit, Wolfe the urbanite would take trips to rural or wild spaces (including the Pennsylvania Dutch farmland, the Hudson River region north of New York City, and the national parks of the West), visit friends in the country (Olin Dows on the Hudson, Elizabeth Lemmon in Middleburg, Virginia), and vacation at mountain cabins (at Oteen, near Asheville; at Anne Armstrong's place in Bristol, Virginia) and seaside cottages (at Orr's Island and Ocean Point, both in Maine).[13] At the same time, while the country affords a larger dose of nature to the city-dweller than he experiences in his urban surroundings, Wolfe makes it clear in his texts that, regardless of where you live, the possibility of at least temporary physical and spiritual restoration is always accessible to those who are sensually drawn to the weather and the seasons.

Given his love of nature, Wolfe was disheartened and sickened wherever he saw the earth being despoiled. Even from his urban vantage point, he noted, "We have done very little for the Hudson except to decorate it with sugar refineries and oil tanks" (*MOL*, 201). In the following comment he gave to the *Asheville Daily News* (May 7, 1937), Wolfe also demonstrates that while he liked to conceive the American landscape in limitless terms, he realized that its natural resources were, in fact, finite:

> I grew up with the idea that America was vast and illimitable and that we could never be milked dry. The bitter reality has dawned in recent years

through floods, dust storms, and erosion that we must pioneer in a new constructive way. We must conserve our resources wisely and think for the welfare of our posterity. (Magi and Walser, 89)

With these sobering environmental realities in mind, Wolfe provides a grim vision in his texts of what is happening to the land without sufficient conservationist safeguards. In "The Hills Beyond," for instance, the narrator surveys the destruction of Zebulon's natural landscape at the hands of greedy developers. In the process, Wolfe dramatizes what he meant when he referred to the land as being "milked"; not only are resources depleted, but the land is made ugly:

> The great mountain slopes and forests of the section had been ruinously detimbered; the farm-soil on hill sides had eroded and washed down; high up, upon the hills, one saw the raw scars of old mica pits, the dump heaps of deserted mines. Some vast destructive "Suck" had been at work here; and a visitor, had he returned after one hundred years, would have been compelled to note the ruin of the change. It was evident that a huge compulsive greed had been at work: the whole region had been sucked and gutted, milked dry, denuded of its rich primeval treasures: something blind and ruthless had been here, grasped, and gone. The blind scars on the hills, the denuded slopes, the empty mica pits were what was left. (*HB*, 183)

Similarly, when George Webber visits his old hometown of Libya Hill, he sees that land is now a commodity, not a resource for life, and that the "development" of the earth and the buying and selling of lots has become the consuming pastime of the townspeople. Moreover, not only does Wolfe suggest that the townspeople had committed a sacrilege when, in seeking further plots, "they had rushed out into the wilderness, into the lyrical immensities of the wild earth where there was land enough for all living men" (114), but that their effort to fence in nature is a ludicrous, hubristic, and futile exercise: "they had staked off little plots and wedges in the hills as one might try to stake a picket fence out in the middle of the ocean" (114). In addition to commodifying the earth, the locals have also, as in Zebulon, despoiled it. In describing the degradation of "a [formerly] beautiful green hill, opulent with rich lawns and lordly trees, with beds of flowers and banks of honeysuckle" (91), Wolfe uses martial language to figure this transformation as a war-like assault against the peaceable beauty of the earth: "It had been one of the pleasantest places in the town, but now it was gone. An army of men and shovels had advanced upon this beautiful green hill and leveled it down to an ugly flat of clay, and had paved it with a desolate horror of white concrete" (*YCGHA*, 91). Even in his first novel, *Look Homeward, Angel*, Wolfe has Eugene notice, from his vantage point above his hometown, the aesthetic distance which separates Altamont's constructed environment from its green spaces: "And about the Square was the treeless brick jungle of business—cheap, ragged, and ugly, and beyond this, in indefinite patches, the houses where all the people lived, with little bright raw ulcers of suburbia far off, *and the healing and concealing grace of fair massed trees*" [emphasis mine] (375). Here, nature's presence is felt as both redemptive ("healing") and beatific ("grace") when juxtaposed to the human-made space of the town. However, Wolfe also suggests that the earth can be redeemed by people who care for it as a source of life, not lucre. One such character is George Webber's friend, Nebraska Crane, a professional baseball player who is planning to retire and farm his acreage near Libya Hill. As the local businessmen try to cajole him into buying up plots of land for real estate profit, Nebraska politely demurs, valuing the earth, instead, as the necessary foundation for building a simple but honest life:

> As Nebraska talked to them in his simple, homely way, he spoke as a man of the earth for whom the future opened up serenely, an independent, stubborn man who knew what he wanted, a man who was firmly rooted. . . . The others talked incessantly about land, but George saw that Nebraska Crane was the only one who still conceived of the land as a place on which to live, and of living on the land as a way of life. (*YCGHA*, 67–68)

Despite Wolfe's lamentations over humanity's abuse of the natural world, he nevertheless viewed the earth as all-conquering in the end. Thus, in addressing the Spanish explorers' plundering of land in "The Men of Old Catawba," he scores their arrogance and notes that the earth will survive both them and their depredations:

> Their next act was to "take possession" of this land in the name of the King of Spain, and to ground the flag. As we read to-day of this solemn ceremony, its pathos and puny arrogance touch us with pity. For what else can we feel for this handful of greedy adventurers "taking

possession" of the immortal wilderness. . . . For the earth is never "taken possession of": it possesses. (*FDTM*, 190–91)

In fact, Wolfe's texts are replete with passages which assert the hegemony of the earth over humanity's pretensions. In *Antaeus, or A Memory of Earth* (1996), Wolfe notes that "by slow tides and secret movings of dark time the dust of our cities melts into the earth: it will possess and drink itself the bones of the cities, the ruins of great towers and ten million streets" (48); and, in the story of the flood, Wolfe has Furman marvel at the folly of those who think they can stem a river's might by building levees:

> "Why, hell-fire!" Furman said, "she'll hit that thing so hard some day they'll never know what struck it. Why, Christ! they might as well dump all those sandbags in the ocean fer all the good it's goin' to do them. Why, woman, that's a *River!*" Furman said, just like he owned it an' was proud of it. "She'll straighten out that bend some day, an' make a new one." (69–70)

Ultimately, the earth and its natural processes are as enduring and invincible as spring itself; in time, flowers will always overwhelm concrete:

> under the pavements trembling like a pulse, under the buildings trembling like a cry, under the waste of time, under the hoof of the beast above the broken bones of cities, there will be something growing like a flower, something bursting from the earth again, forever deathless, faithful, coming into life again like April. (*YCGHA*, 40)

Given Wolfe's faith in the earth's resiliency, the tragedy of Libya Hill is measured less in the loss of earth than in the loss of a way of life, a life that is grounded in nature. It is this that he has in mind when he concludes, with Biblical and prophetic overtones, "They had ruined their city, and in doing so had ruined themselves, their children, and their children's children" (*YCGHA*, 114). This dire assertion also suggests the extent to which Wolfe saw a connection between the denaturing of the land and the vulgarization of life. When George Webber revisits his hometown cemetery, its unspoiled innocence—"There was the last evening cry of robins, and the thrumming bullet noises in undergrowth and leaf. . . . There was the fragrance of intoxicating odors—the resinous smell of pine, and the smells of grass and warm sweet clover. All this was just as it had always been" (116)—reminds him of how his life, and the former lifestyle of the community, had been inseparable from nature while he was growing up. And it had been a better life. Rather than being jarred by the discordant sounds of earth movers, as the town's collective consciousness now was, it had previously been synchronous with the rustling of leaves:

> But the town of his childhood, with its quiet streets and the old houses which had been almost obscured below the leafy spread of trees, was changed past recognition, scarred now with hard patches of bright concrete and raw clumps of new construction. . . . And in the interspaces only the embowered remnants of the old and pleasant town remained— timid, retreating, overwhelmed—to remind one of the liquid shuffle in the quiet streets at noon when the men came home to lunch, and of laughter and low voices in the leafy rustle of the night. For this was lost! (116)

David Herbert Donald has seized on this type of social commentary as an ecological statement about the spiritual wasteland of the 1930s: "Long before most American intellectuals were involved in the ecology movement, Wolfe connected the disorders of the American spirit with the violation of the natural environment" (*Look Homeward*, 437). The implied connections between culture and environment in Wolfe's fiction are the combined result of his perceptive reading of human character and his belief that human beings can be fully understood only if they are treated as both creatures and creators of their environments. As a result, he was adept at reading signs of the environment in human behavior and, conversely, reading signs of human behavior in the environment. In surveying the cultural and environmental landscapes of the 1930s, Wolfe saw a pervasive and insidious "machine in the garden" at work, with the automobile as its avatar:[14]

> The feeling returned to him . . . that "something" had come into life, "something new" which he could not define, but something that was disturbing and sinister, and which was somehow represented by the powerful, weary, and inhuman precision of these great, glittering, stamped-out beetles of machinery. (*OTR*, 592)

As a result of the modern style and tempo of living, as embodied by machines, "something new" had also insinuated itself into people's very substance: "They were, in short, the faces of people who had been hurled ten thousand times through the roaring darkness of a subway tunnel" (593). Ultimately, these machines had been complicit in alienating people from the earth; people had "hurtled down the harsh and brutal ribbons of their concrete roads at such savage speeds that now the earth was lost forever, and they never saw the earth again" (593). Theirs had become a "mechanic life" (898). Until he died, Wolfe remained adamant in his view that separation from the earth yields dehumanization; it was, for him, a self-evident corollary.

Still, nature was never dormant for Wolfe, and its quickening presence reassured him that America was still vital at its cultural and organic roots despite the scourges of modern ills. In a time of dislocation, emblematized by the Great Depression, there was comfort, for Wolfe, in the bedrock certainty, eternality, integrity, preeminence, and life-affirming substance of nature: "He [Eugene] felt suddenly the devastating impermanence of the nation. Only the earth endured—the gigantic American earth, bearing upon its awful breast a world of flimsy rickets" (*LHA*, 352). Ultimately, intones Wolfe, "All things that lapse and change and come again upon the earth—these things will always be the same, for they come from the earth that never changes, they go back into the earth that lasts forever. Only the earth endures, but it endures forever" (*YCGHA*, 40). In fact, it was this same faith in nature that most separated him from his contemporaries; it enabled him to see spring amid the modernist winter and, in his writing process, led him to tap the wellspring of nature within himself.

Thus, while Wolfe often figures nature in his texts as an indifferent force in a naturalistic universe, he also treats nature's mountains, rivers, stones, and leaves ("a stone, a leaf, a door") as the talismanic articles of Eugene Gant's and George Webber's secular faith.[15] Ultimately, suggests Wolfe, nature's architecture is an omnipresent and tangible reminder to humans that they inhabit a larger, nonhuman stage, live out their destinies under the aegis of the earth and the sky. It is this metaphysical reality that Wolfe has in mind when, in the same scene in *Of Time and the River* where Eugene and his friends are traveling to Boston on a train, Wolfe pointedly observes that each of these youths is "sure that his destiny is written in the blazing stars, his life shone over by the fortunate watches of the moon, his fame nourished or sustained by the huge earth, whose single darling charge he is, on whose immortal stillness he is flung onward in the night" (68).

Thomas Wolfe loved mountains, but he was certainly not a mountain man—despite the fact he played such a character in one of his own plays.[16] In fact, he was a hill-born man who became addicted to the city. Yet, he never felt entirely at ease in the city because he felt alienated from the earth there.[17] Despite his urban vantage point, however, he continued to be a watcher of nature and to seek refreshment in natural settings. He also maintained a reverence for the nonhuman world, as evidenced when he visited the redwoods with a friend from Palo Alto, Dr. Russel V. Lee, and greeted the ancient trees in a way that would have pleased John Muir himself: "Dr. Lee took Wolfe to see the giant redwoods in the Sequoia National Park. Finding them 'the most satisfactory thing he had ever seen in nature,' he stood in rapt admiration for an hour and, for once in his life, was utterly silent" (Donald, *Look Homeward,* 339). This is the same Wolfe who is captured in a photo feeding a chipmunk during his national parks tour. Dressed in his rumpled suit, he gently and patiently watches the animal feed itself on his lap (Morton I. Teicher, *Looking Homeward: A Thomas Wolfe Photo Album,* 149). This is also the same Wolfe who, at 37, became excited by the sight of cornfields in Virginia: "I remember how he kept pointing to the cornfields we passed, the corn in shock now. 'Corn!' he exclaimed, in a low voice, several times. 'Corn—the most American thing in America!'" (Armstrong, "As I Saw Thomas Wolfe," 13–14). At his core, then, and despite his self-exile in cities, he remained a person whose spirit always yearned for the freeing and quickening pulse of the natural world.

In a brief comment inserted into a long letter to Aline Bernstein (Winter, 1932), Wolfe notes that his mother had just visited him and that he felt as if his contact with her earthy nature had given back his life: "My mother's visit here literally saved my life. I got back to the earth again, and to a sense of reality and having roots" (*MOL,* 345). Like Antaeus, Wolfe was strengthened by Mother Earth; like Eugene Gant and George Webber, it was his touchstone.

Chapter Four

Invoking Nature's Presence

Methods and Effects

Wolfe does much more than merely draw attention to the nonhuman world in his texts. More significantly, he dramatizes the *relationship* that exists between people and nature by placing his characters within a textual field of nature observations, language, references, and images, all serving to convey, interdependently, the overarching, encompassing, and interpenetrating presence of nature in human lives. In addition, just as nature affords Wolfe's protagonists a "still point" in their otherwise chaotic lives, so do his nature references provide, collectively, a "still point" in his narratives, that is, a recurring source of constancy which constitutes the structural anchor of a Wolfe novel. The overall greening of his oeuvre, then, is based not on the sheer volume of his nature references but, instead, on nature cues that are strategically placed and both rhetorical and structural in design.[1]

Perhaps Wolfe's most obvious greening device is the dramatic placement of his story lines within the context of the seasons, the ur-text of nature's cycle: "That Spring—in the green sorcery of that final, fatal, and ruinous April—a madness which was compounded of many elements took possession of him" (*WR*, 499); "April passed, and May came on, and there was neither change nor hope of change in Monk" (554). In the special case of the spring images which open chapter sixteen of *Look Homeward, Angel*, Wolfe's "seasonalizing" not only casts a vernal atmosphere over the ensuing narrative, but also makes us aware—through the "split-screen" presentation of spring alongside the human action—that nature's own "dramas" are ceaseless, ever-present, and independent of us:

> The Spring grew ripe. There was at mid-day a soft drowsiness in the sun. Warm spurting gusts of wind howled faintly at the eaves; the young grass bent; the daisies twinkled.
>
> He [Eugene] pressed his high knees uncomfortably against the bottom of his desk, grew nostalgic on his dreams. Bessie Barnes scrawled vigorously two rows away, displaying her long full silken leg. (170)

Not only are human affairs framed by the seasons, but they are keyed to them as well; thus, the "seasonalization" of George Webber's relationship with Esther Jack:

> They lived their lives out like the seasons, giving to each its due:
>
> To Spring, all of the leaping and the dancing, the flashing of young forms in silver pools, the hunt, the capture, and the race.
>
> To Summer, battle, the swift thud of mighty flesh, victory without pity or injustice, defeat without resignation.
>
> Then to October they brought all their grain of wisdom, their ripe deliberation. Their calm eyes saw a few things that endured—the sea, the mountain, and the sky—and they walked together, talking with grave gestures of the fate of man. . . .
>
> When December came, without lamentings in the room, but by the wall and quietly, they turned their grey heads tranquilly below their robes, and died. (WR, 554–55)

There is also, for Wolfe, a seasonal substratum to human character, a reminder that humans *are* nature incarnate. Thus, Miss Brill, the typist in Bascom Pentland's office, is characterized "as always unfastening her galoshes" because

> some people inevitably belong to seasons, and this girl's season was winter—not blizzards or howling winds, or the blind skirl and sweep of snow, but gray, grim, raw, thick, implacable winter: the endless successions of gray days and gray monotony. There was no spark of color in her, her body was somewhat thick and heavy, her face was white, dull, and thick-featured. (OTR, 116)

Given Wolfe's implicit belief that his stories were "groundless" unless fitted with seasonal foundations, and given his primal and visceral responses to "the royal processional of the months" (LHA, 249), his seasonal consciousness can appear paganish. In fact, he often figures the coming of spring in mythological terms; it is, he suggests, "the month when Prosperpine comes back, and Ceres' dead heart rekindles, when all the woods are a tender smoky blur" (78); and it is also the time when "the young gods loiter: they hear the reed, the oatenstop, the running goat-hoofs in the spongy wood, here, there, everywhere: they dawdle, listen . . . because the earth is full of ancient rumor and they cannot find the way" (78). Although these passages represent nature dressed up with art, the ubiquitous references to the seasons in Wolfe's texts suggest that he literally, not just figuratively, viewed the ebb and flow of human life as being confluent with the organic rhythms of the earth.

Not only can Wolfe's characters become "lost" in nature ("the earth is full of ancient rumor and they cannot find the way"), but they can also become lost in the "overgrowth" of his nature rhetoric, which serves to draw attention to nature and away from human events. This dynamic is famously illustrated in chapter thirty-nine in *Of Time and the River*, where the dramaturgical voice of Eugene Gant, in the protracted "October had come again" monologue, elegizes Eugene's deceased father by drawing on metaphors from nature and invoking October images:

> All things in earth point home again in old October. . . . all things that live upon this earth return, return: Father, will you not, too, come back again? . . . .
>
> Father, . . . In the night, in the dark, I have heard the howling of the winds among the great trees, and the sharp and windy raining of the acorns. In the night, in the dark, I have heard the feet of rain upon the roofs, the glut and gurgle of the gutter spouts, and the soaking gulping throat of all the mighty earth. . . .
>
> Come to us, Father, in the watches of the night. . . . Come to us, Father, while the winds howl in the darkness, for October has come again bringing with it huge prophecies of death and life. . . . For we are ruined, lost, and broken if you do not come, and our lives, like rotten chips, are whirled about us onward in darkness to the sea. (332–33)

During the course of this extended litany of nature references, Eugene's felt presence diminishes as the land and the weather become foreground. To similar effect, Wolfe "frontloads" the following passage with so much nature imagery that the human action ("Eliza moved into Dixieland") is represented almost as an afterthought: "In the young autumn when the maples were still full and green, and the migratory swallows filled secretly the trees with clamor, and swooped of an evening in a black whirlwind down, drifting at its funnel end, like dead leaves, into their chosen chimney, Eliza moved into Dixieland" (*LHA*, 106). Accordingly, Wolfe's nature descriptions often end up supplanting, imagistically, the would-be centrality of the protagonist's "place" in the text; that is, Wolfe ends up supplanting an anthropocentric perspective with an ecocentric one, with the nonhuman world appearing to overwhelm the human world both figuratively and textually.

By contrast, there are sections in Wolfe's texts where nature scenes play off human scenes in contrapuntal fashion, the effect of which is to suggest that the human and the nonhuman are engaged in a relationship. More-over, a *prolonged* series of such "interactions" tends to further suggest an *inter*relationship, as human and nonhuman scenes appear to become con-founded. In addition, the fact that nature scenes appear to "co-opt" human scenes can also foster the added impression that the nonhuman world "contains" the human world. An example of this interplay is found in chapter fourteen of *Look Homeward, Angel,* which chronicles the awakening of Altamont. The chapter begins, "The plum-tree, black and brittle, rocks stiffly in winter wind. . . . But in the Spring, lithe and heavy, she will bend under her great load of fruit and blossoms" (137). Subsequently, Wolfe weaves local observations of nature—especially the transition from "lilac" to "pearl" light as the land and sky metamorphose from nighttime to day-time—over, around, and alongside the Joycean vignettes of various towns-folk: "The night is brightly pricked with cool and tender stars. The orchard stirs leafily in the short fresh wind. Ben prowls softly out of the sleeping house" (137); "By the cool orchards in the dark the paper-carriers go. The copper legs of negresses in their dark dens stir. The creek brawls cleanly" (138); "Spring lay strewn lightly like a fragrant gauze upon the earth; the night was a cool bowl of lilac darkness, filled with fresh orchard scents" (139); "Strangely, in sharp fragments, life awoke in the lilac darkness" (140); "Nacreous pearl light swam faintly about the hem of the lilac dark-ness; the edges of light were stitched upon the hills. Morning moved like a pearl-gray tide across the fields and up the hill-flanks, flowing rapidly into the soluble dark" (144); "Bull-lunged, their laughter filled the nacreous dawn" (145); "The light that filled the world now was soft and other-worldly like the light that fills the sea-floors of Catalina where the great fish swam. Flat-footedly . . . Patrolman Leslie Roberts . . . slouched through the submarine light" (145); "The four medical men went out into the pearl light. The town emerged from the lilac darkness with a washed renascent cleanliness. All the world seemed as young as Spring" (149); "Virginal sun-light crept into the street in young moteless shafts. At this moment Gant woke up" (150); "Sister Theresa, the Mother Superior, walked softly through the dormitory lifting the window-shade beside each cot, letting the orchard cherry-apple bloom come gently into the long cool glade of roseleaf sleeping girls" (155). The woven appearance of these contiguous human and nonhuman images creates the impression of interconnection and inseparability between Altamont's citizens and nature. Finally, the same plum tree which opens this chapter also closes it ("Eugene, . . . waking suddenly to Gant's powerful command from the foot of the stairs, turned his face full into a momentary vision of roseflushed blue sky and tender blossoms that drifted slowly earthward" [158]), thus enclosing the intervening human action, suggesting, textually, that the human world is also situated *within* nature. Thus, the tree's blossoms seem to cast their "roseflushed" magic over all of Altamont, illuminating with nature-borne beauty the otherwise prosaic lives of the townspeople.[2]

Similarly, in two successive chapters in *Look Homeward, Angel,* Wolfe uses a series of references to the wind, October, birds waking, and leaves shaking to frame Ben's death as an organic event that is both part of, and situated within, the transcendent, affirmative, and vital life of nature. The repeated references, which have the effect of a liturgical chant, begin right after Ben dies, in the first section of chapter thirty-six—"In that enormous silence, where pain and darkness met, some birds were waking. It was October. It was almost four o'clock in the morning. Eliza straightened out Ben's limbs, and folded his hands across his body" (465); "The leaves were quaking. Some birds began to chatter in the trees. Wind pressed the boughs, the withered leaves were shaking. It was October" (469)—and are reprised in the last section of chapter thirty-seven: "Wind pressed the boughs, the withered leaves were shaking. It was October, but the leaves were shaking" (486). Juxtaposed to the climate of grief associated with Ben's death, these choric references serve to contextualize his dying as an inextricable part of the organic process of all life and to invoke a sort of Emersonian Oversoul: "But over us all, over us all, over us all, is something. Wind pressed the boughs; the withered leaves were shaking" (486).

Another such contrapuntal use of nature is found in the section of *The Web and the Rock* where a verbal exchange between two lovers is counterpointed by a rustling of leaves across America: "And the rustle of young leaves across America, and, 'Say it!' . . . and the leaves softly, 'say it, say it'— and half-yielding, desperate, fierce, 'Then . . . if you promise!'—the leaves, then sighing, 'promise, promise'" (441).[3] With nature serving here as an echo chamber for human voices, Wolfe suggests not only that a "dialogue" is taking place between the human and nonhuman worlds, but that nature is so encompassing that it engages with us all the time, even when we are not aware of its presence.

Yet another section which utilizes a nature refrain is Eugene's train journey out of the South in *Of Time and the River*. In this case, nature—in the form of repeated references to the moonscapes of both Virginia ("outside, . . . the old earth of Virginia now lay dreaming in the moon's white light" [68]) and the American continent ("The moon blazed down upon the vast desolation of the American coasts" [72])—interpenetrates and punctuates the horseplay, splintered dialogues, and drunken revelry of Eugene and his mates:

> lay dreaming in the moonlight, beaming in the moonlight, seeming in the moonlight, to be dreaming to be gleaming in the moon.
> —Give 'em hell, son!
> —Here, give him another drink! —Attaboy! Drink her down!
> —Drink her down—drink her down—drink her down—damn your soul—drink her down!
> —By God, I'll drink her down. . . .
> Lay dreaming in the moonlight, beaming in the moonlight, to be seeming to be beaming in the moonlight moonlight moonlight oonlight oonlight oonlight oonlight oonlight.
> And Virginia lay dreaming in the moon. (71–72)

The result of this back and forth image-making is that, cast in the moon's lyrical and dreamy magic, the boys become part of, rather than apart from, the natural world outside the train: "The moon steeped all the earth in its living and unearthly substance" (72).[4]

References in this same section to "the dream-charged moon-enchanted mind" (75) and "the moon-haunted and dream-tortured faces of the sleepers" (75) also demonstrate Wolfe's method of bringing nature into his texts via *mind*scapes (thoughts, recollections, even dreams), thus suggesting the interpenetration of human consciousness by the organic world. For example, as Gant lies dying in *Of Time and the River*, he revisits in a dream the familiar rural landscape of his childhood. Having resigned himself to his own dying process, "without weariness or anxiety, and with a perfect and peaceful acquiescence" (*OTR,* 256), he envisions an equally peaceful bucolic scene where even the suggestive graveyard becomes a site of beauty within a pastoral tableau:

> Towards one o'clock that night Gant fell asleep and dreamed that he was walking down the road that led to Spangler's Run. . . . It was a fine morning in early May and everything was sweet and green and as familiar as it had always been. The graveyard was carpeted with thick green grass, and all around the graveyard and the church there was the incomparable green velvet of young wheat. And the thought came back to Gant, as it had come to him a thousand times, that the wheat around the graveyard looked greener and richer than any other wheat that he had ever seen. (258)

Perhaps Wolfe's most "spectacular" device for dramatizing humanity's place within nature is his use of aerial "shots" of the landscape, views which are recorded by both narrators and protagonists and which can be actual or visionary. Thus, in *The Web and the Rock,* the narrator speaks of the "whole design and pattern of the earth which had grown so complete and radiant in [George Webber's] mind that sometimes in the night he thought he saw it all stretched out upon the canvas of his vision—hills, mountains, plains, and deserts" (562). A similarly telescopic vision enables the narrator of *You Can't Go Home Again* to survey the country in miniature from atop the Rocky Mountains ("Turn now, seeker, on your resting stool atop the Rocky Mountains, and look another thousand miles or so across moon-blazing fiend-worlds of the Painted Desert and beyond Sierra's ridge" [391]); and, while Eugene is gazing at the dreamy moonlight of Virginia, Wolfe moves his visual camera high above not only Virginia, but America itself, providing a perspective which dwarfs the human drama being played out "on the ground" below: "The moon blazed down on 18,000 miles of coast, on the million sucks and scoops and hollows of the shore, and on the great wink of the sea" (*OTR,* 72). Wolfe uses this same distance-spanning lens when, in relating how the townsfolk of Altamont use telegraph reports to construct the course of a baseball game being played in "the North," he focuses on the topographical expanse which separates the two events, an optical maneuver which causes the game to become "lost" in the convolutions of the land. This is also another case of

framing human action ("the lean right arm of the great pitcher Mathew-
son is flashing like a whip") from an ecocentric perspective by frontload-
ing a passage with nature rhetoric:

> somewhere across the illimitable fields and folds and woods and hills
> and hollows of America, across the huge brown earth, the mown fields,
> the vast wild space, the lavish, rude and unfenced distances, the famil-
> iar, homely, barren, harsh, strangely haunting scenery of the nation;
> somewhere through the crisp, ripe air . . . the lean right arm of the great
> pitcher Mathewson is flashing like a whip. (*OTR,* 202)

In all these scenic overviews, it is as if Wolfe, as film director, felt com-
pelled to dramatize how, from a more cosmic viewpoint, humans and their
artifacts become diminished by land masses, oceans, and lakes. From such
heights, it is easier to comprehend how the earth may be said to "house"
humanity, an impression fostered to great effect when Wolfe pans across
the American continent in the opening scene of *The Hound of Darkness*
(1986). Here, the initial "shot" appears as if it were taken from a spaceship,
revealing "the body and bones of the American continent" (3); "the spec-
tator to this giant panorama sees at once and instantly the whole dimension of the nation, spread out in the essential lineaments of a gigantic
map." Eerily, the land appears lifeless and alien from such a height: "The
view in this first instant is appalling—it seems crater-blasted, lifeless and
inhuman, like the design and landscape of a prehistoric world"; "At first
nothing seems to move or live or stir upon this surface." As the camera
slowly closes in, however, the landscape becomes more defined: "Rising
from piedmont swell and coastal plain, the ancient ramified embankment
of the Appalachian range extends for fifteen hundred miles from New
Hampshire into Georgia" (4). As "the vision nears and deepens," the
sounds of the sea are picked up and, later, the sound of a train. Subsequently, the camera focuses more narrowly still on "a country road in Illi-
nois" (5), where "the moon burns brightly on an unpaved road that goes
straight as a string between two walls of corn." A "dusty Buick, model
1912" appears, then vanishes, leaving, at the end of the scene, the motionless corn and the "moon-white . . . silence of the road again." Even after
closing the visual distance from outer space to an eye-level view of a road
with a car on it, Wolfe's lingering view is of nature. In the end, the
"machine" disappears into the "garden."

Given that most of the action in Wolfe's narratives after *Look Homeward, Angel* occurs in city settings, it is especially revealing to see how he not only brings nature "into" these ostensibly inorganic environments, but also creates the impression that nature is as much an overarching presence there as it is in rural settings. In *The Modern American Urban Novel: Nature as "Interior Structure"* (1991), Arnold Goldsmith challenges Blanche Gelfant's assertion that language drawn from nature is "incongruous" in a city novel: "American [urban] novelists from Dos Passos to Bellow *have* drawn 'heavily upon metaphors and symbols from nature,' and the resulting contrast serves multiple purposes and strategies that greatly enhance their work" (11). Goldsmith further suggests that not only have certain city novelists used literal and figurative references to nature to tell their stories, but that they have also treated nature as "neither [a] principal character nor mere backdrop, but an integral part of the setting, language, symbolism, and even characterization" (10). Wolfe's fiction aptly illustrates this "green" treatment of city-based narratives. For example, Wolfe's observations of nature in country settings seem at times to overwhelm the felt presence of his protagonists (and humanity in general), so do his many city-based observations of nature seem at times to displace the felt presence of the city. This dynamic is illustrated in the following passage where George Webber notes, from his city purview, how certain seasons elicit epiphanic moments of "exuberance and joy" (*WR*, 221):

> In New York there are certain wonderful seasons in which this feeling grows to lyrical intensity. One of these are those first tender days of Spring when lovely girls and women seem suddenly to burst out of the pavements like flowers. . . . Another season is early Autumn, in October, when the city begins to take on a magnificent flash and sparkle: there are swift whippings of bright wind, a flare of bitter leaves, the smell of frost and harvest in the air; after the enervation of Summer, the place awakens to an electric vitality. . . .
>
> Finally, there is a wonderful, secret thrill of some impending ecstasy on a frozen winter's night. On one of these nights of frozen silence when the cold is so intense that it numbs one's flesh . . . the whole city . . . becomes a proud, passionate, Northern place. (221)

In a reversal of the standard treatment of the city and nature—where nature serves as an urban backdrop only—here the seasons are rendered transcendent as the human-made habitat becomes naturalized amid the leaves, wind, and frost, and, in the process, acquires a seasonal personae. In any case, this "seasonalizing" of the city not only adds greater vibrancy to the urban landscape, but greater piquancy to seasonal images as well. While there is magic in the greening of the once-brown earth, there is an especial magic in the greening of gray pavement, gray faces, and gray spirits: "Not the whole glory of the great plantation of the earth could have outdone the glory of the city streets that Spring. Neither the cry of the great, green fields, nor the song of the hills . . . could have surpassed the wordless and poignant glory of a single tree in a city street that Spring" (WR, 409).

Whether or not Wolfe draws on imagistic effects to dress the city in a green mantle, he views urban spaces as being as much exposed to, and influenced by, nature as is any rural setting. The moonlight that falls on the Virginia landscape is the same that falls on Boston as Eugene and Starwick saunter joyfully through the city streets at night: "Above them, in the cool sweet skies of night, the great moons of the springtime, and New England, blazed with a bare, a lovely and enchanted radiance. And around them the great city, and its thousand narrow twisted streets lay anciently asleep beneath that blazing moon" (OTR, 280). Moreover, the nights can be just as cold and starry in urban spaces as in the backwoods, and the stars themselves can be no less a balm to city onlookers than they are to those lying on their backs in country meadows:

> Sometimes, on a cold still night in winter, the sky had the peculiar frosty clarity that comes from a still, biting cold. Above the great vertical radiance and cold Northern passion of New York, it was a-glitter with magnificent stars . . . and as Eugene looked his weariness was cleansed out of him at once . . . he drank the air into his veins in great gulps. (OTR, 443)

Similarly, the sun that "went glistering" (LHA, 380) in Laura's hair in the "timeless valley" near Altamont is the same sun that irradiates Esther on a city sidewalk, a sidewalk where a tree grows, miraculously, like a stolen treasure from an alien green world:

> They had paused beneath a slender tree, one of the few along the street: it grew up from a lonely scrap of earth wedged in between an old brick house and the grey pavement: and through young boughs, now leaved with the first smoky green of the year, the sun cast a net of dancing

spangles on the wide brim of Esther's hat and the rich green of the dress she wore, swarming in moths of golden light upon her straight, small shoulders. (*WR*, 548)

Wolfe's characters are also no less alert to the signs of nature in the city than in the country. Even the jaded urbanite, C. Green, is mindful of the seasonal cycle amid the static, constructed landscape all around him: "In March there is a day that's almost spring, and C. Green, strong with will to have it so, says, 'Well, it's here'—and it is gone like smoke" (*YCGHA*, 361). Brooklynite George Webber evinces a more acute—and rhapsodic— eco-consciousness based on his basement-level view of a tree outside his apartment; the tree serves as his lifeline to the earth, the seasons, and the sights and sounds of nature:

> But he found beauty in South Brooklyn, too. There was a tree that leaned over into the narrow alley where he lived, and George could stand at his basement window and look up at it and watch it day by day as it came into its moment's glory of young and magic green. And then toward sun-set . . . he could . . . listen to the dying birdsong in the tree. Thus, each spring, in that one tree, he found all April and the earth. (*YCGHA*, 336)[5]

In fact, whether it is "a single tree in a city street" or a tree in an alley (a motif he recycles in *You Can't Go Home Again, The Web and the Rock, From Death to Morning,* and other texts), Wolfe often uses city trees as transcendent metaphors for all of nature. His city trees especially herald "the first green of the year, and particularly the first green in the city" (*WR* 500), a greening which is able to change the very atmosphere of the city, "drawing all the swarming chaos and confusion of the city into one great lyrical harmony of life."

Ironically, despite the fact that cities offer micro-settings of nature in the form of urban gardens, parks, zoos, rivers, and ponds, Wolfe rarely uses these habitats in his texts. When he does use them, however, they serve as green interludes, sensual respites from the overwhelming sight of inorganic, human-wrought artifacts and surroundings. One such example is the scene in *Of Time and the River* where Starwick and Eugene walk along the Charles River: "Spring had come with the sudden, almost explosive loveliness that marks its coming in New England: along the banks of the river the birch trees leaned their slender, white and beautiful trunks, and their boughs were coming swiftly into the young and tender green of

May" (309). In effect, this passage insinuates a patch of green into the "middle" of a predominantly non-green section of the text in the same way that the Charles and its natural environs inhabit the "middle" of Boston. Perhaps the most compelling and poignant instance of Wolfe's use of nature to signal a green interlude in a city-based narrative can be found in the short story, "In the Park." Here, young Esther Jack recalls an evening with her father and his friends. They begin the evening at a play, move on to a restaurant for dinner, and end up taking a car ride in the early morning around Central Park. Given that all of the preceding action has taken place indoors, the park scene functions in the text as a breath of fresh air. In fact, the rich images of nature gradually crowd out the human story while also serving, metaphorically, as an outward expression of little Esther's ecstatic feelings:

> It was just the beginning of May, and all the leaves and buds were coming out; they had that tender feathery look, and there was just a little delicate shaving of moon in the sky, and it was so cool and lovely, with the smell of the leaves, and the new grass, and all the flowers bursting from the earth til you could hear them grow: it seemed to me the loveliest thing I had ever known. (*FDTM*, 182–83)

As Esther goes on to recall the waking sounds of birds, the city "outside" the park further recedes from her sight and consciousness. At this point, the language of nature becomes lyrical and onomatopoeic, effectively drowning out the human noises of the city as nature speaks the last word:

> and then dawn came, and all the birds began to sing. Now broke the birdsong in first light, and suddenly I heard each sound the birdsong made: like a flight of shot, the sharp fast skaps of sound arose. With chitterling bicker, fast-fluttering skirrs of sound, the palmy, honeyed birdcries came. Smooth drops and nuggets of bright gold they were. Now sang the birdtree filled with lutings in bright air: the thrum, the lark's wing, and tongue-trilling chirrs arose now. And now the little brainless cries arose, with liquorous, liquified lutings, with lirruping chirp, plumbellied smoothness, sweet lucidity. And now I heard the rapid kweet-kweet-kweet-kweet-kweet of homely birds, and then their pwee-pwee-pwee . . . and it was just like that, and the sun came up, and it was like the first day of the world. (183–84)

By the end of this passage, the reader can just as easily imagine that he has been listening to birdsong from the front steps of a forest cabin. In fact, Esther Jack's green vision, whether as a child or an adult, itself constitutes a green interlude in Wolfe's city. Esther's special gift is that, rather than seeing the greenness in the city as a composite of scenic fragments, she sees the city whole as an inherently green place: "No, for Mrs. Jack the city was her living tenement; it was her field, her pasture, and her farm" (*WR*, 364). As a child, her green vision had been so compelling that the sailing ships in New York had appeared to her "like a forest of young trees, they were delicate and spare and close together and they had no leaves upon them and [she] thought of Spring" (381). Being still loyal to her childhood vision of the city, Esther passionately tells George Webber

> that the earth is here, and that we knew it [as children]. This is the soil, the harvest, and the earth. I tell you there has never been an earth more potent and more living than these streets and pavements. . . . This was my meadow. I knew it and I loved it, I walked about in it, these faces were my blades of grass. (632).

Wolfe also uses his aerial camera to expose the overriding green context of urban spaces, to convey the impression that all the life stories in a city are transpiring within a larger environment than the immediate, street level milieu of cars, concrete, and lampposts. From this perspective, he dramatizes how New York City—bounded by the earth below, the rivers and ocean at ground level, and the sky above—seems constituted of its nonhuman surroundings, and, as a result, appears to merge with them. Encircled by rivers, fronted by the sea, and surmounted by the weather, the air, and the sun, the city is figured as a rock lying atop the earth:

> And the magical and shining air—the strange, subtle and enchanted weather, was above them, and the buried men were strewn through the earth on which they trod, and a bracelet of great tides was flashing round them, and the enfabled rock on which they swarmed swung eastward in the marches of the sun into eternity, and was masted like a ship with its terrific towers, and was flung with a lion's port between its tides into the very maw of the infinite, all-taking ocean. (*OTR*, 417)

Moreover, this rock-city is an anatomical part of the corpus of America:

across the body, bones, sinews, tissues, juices, rivers, mountains, plains, streams, lakes, coastal regions, and compacted corporosity of the American continent, a train might have been observed by one of the lone watchers of the Jersey Flats approaching that enfabled rock. (*WR*, 209)

In fact, Wolfe's protagonists are themselves mindful that the city is ultimately founded on the earth, the "rock" of Manhattan. As Esther Jack reassures herself, "Down below all the pavements and the buildings was the earth. There was nothing down below there but the earth. If all the earth had been completely covered by these pavements, there would still be nothing that endured except the earth" (*WR*, 628). Even Mr. Jack, the hidebound urbanite, consciously acknowledges the earth below from high atop his skyscraper eyrie:

> With fingers pressed against his swelling breast, he breathed in a deep draft of the fresh, living air of morning. It was laden with the thrilling compost of the city, a fragrance delicately blended of many things. There was, strangely, the smell of earth, moist and somehow flowerful, tinged faintly with the salt reek of tidal waters and the fresh river smell, rank and rotten. (*YCGHA*, 123)

Mr. Jack also acknowledges the earth's enduring solidity when he feels his building shaken by the rumbling of the subway, a harbinger of the economy's imminent crash: "he would have liked it better if the building had been anchored upon the solid rock" (*YCGHA*, 124). Thus, in Wolfe's green vision, the city's "rootless pavements" (*OTR*, 424) constitute a false bottom, a superficial, parchment-thin layer between its inhabitants and the bedrock which truly "grounds" them.

While the earth shoulders the city from below, the "maw of the infinite all-taking ocean" fronts the city to the East, suggesting the extent to which the ostensibly outsized human habitat of the city is, itself, dwarfed by the oceanic presence of the natural world. New York is also "contained" by the rivers which encircle it: "there will always be the great rivers flowing around it in the darkness, the rivers that have bounded so many nameless lives, those rivers which have moated in so many changes" (*OTR*, 859–60). In addition to serving as natural boundaries, the rivers also cleanse the city as well as serve as conduits to the earth:

it [the Hudson River] flows there, in the daytime, in the dark, drinking with ceaseless glut the land, mining into its tides the earth . . . foaming about piled crustings of old wharves, sliding like time and silence by the vast cliff of the city . . . thick with the wastes of earth, dark with our stains, and heavied with our dumpings, rich, rank, beautiful, and unending as all life, all living, as it flows by us, by us, by us, to the sea! (510).

Finally, the sky serves the city as both a "roof" and a transfiguring medium. While it backlights the city during the day, making the buildings appear "sky-hung against the crystal of the frail blue weather" (*WR*, 440–41), it seems to undo the outlines of the buildings at night, causing the myriad of electric lights to resemble a sidereal space: "the lights were sown like flung stars. . . . It seemed to him all at once that there was nothing there but the enchanted architecture of the dark, star-sown with a million lights. He forgot the buildings" (440). This stellar figuring of the city is further reinforced when we see it thousands of feet above the earth: "Behold the gem-strung towns and cities of the good, green East, flung like star-dust through the field of night. That spreading constellation to the north is called Chicago" (*YCGHA*, 391). Thus, in the nature-wide scheme of things, the cities of the nation are reduced in scope and grandiosity, resembling "the star-flung crustaceans of the continent" small objects in nature's ocean. (*WR*, 441)

Another method that Wolfe uses to bring the natural world into his city-based narratives is to "import" images from the country, as illustrated when Wolfe draws on images from the New England landscape to describe the advent of fall in Boston:

Outside his uncle's dirty window he could see the edge of Faneuil Hall, and hear the swarming and abundant activity of the markets. . . . For it seemed to him that nowhere more than here was the passionate enigma of New England felt: New England with its harsh and stony soil, and its tragic and lonely beauty; its desolate rocky coasts and its swarming fisheries, the white, piled, frozen bleakness of its winters with the magnificent jewelry of stars, the dark firwoods. (*OTR*, 137)

As a result of this juxtaposition, the city's environmental identity becomes temporarily countrified. This greening effect is similarly reproduced when Wolfe observes how Eugene, in returning to the city from the country, "brought to it the million memories of his fathers who were great men and knew the wilderness, but who had never lived in cities" (413). He also brought to it the memories of these men's voices: "There have been bird-calls for our flesh within the wilderness" (415); "'Who sows the barren earth?' their voices cried. 'We sowed the wilderness with blood and sperm . . . we gave tongue to solitude, a pulse to the desert, the barren earth received us and gave back our agony: we made the earth cry out'" (414). As a result, writes Wolfe, "all that [Eugene] remembered of this earth he brought to the city, and it seemed to be the city's complement—to feed it, to sustain it, to belong to it" (415), thus "seeding" both a greener city in Eugene's mind and a green space in a city-based chapter. Wolfe achieves similar greening effects by strategically interjecting rural-based chapters between city-based chapters. Thus, chapters fifty-eight and sixty-five in *Of Time and the River,* which feature Eugene's visit to the Pierce's pastoral estate on the Hudson, constitute an extensive and densely-packed pastoral interlude which casts a green afterimage over the encompassing city-based narrative.

Wolfe also brings nature into the city by figuring it and its environs in organic terms. The city is, variously, a "rock," a "jungle," and a "web"; the human traffic is a "tide"; the buildings are "cliffs" and "mountains," with "canyons" between them; and a single building is "a giant honeycomb" whose "nerves, bones, and sinews went down below the level of the street" (*YCGHA,* 157).[6] Wolfe also organicizes the city as a plant: "He ate and drank the city to its roots" (416); "To eat you, branch and root and tree; to devour you, golden fruit of power and love and happiness; to consume you to your sources, river and spire and rock, down to your iron roots" (*OTR,* 508), "he felt he could tear the buildings up by the roots like onions from the earth" (*WR,* 504). Guided by this organic perspective, Wolfe not only figures the landscape as so much organic matter, but the inhabitants as well: "The streets were bursting into life again, . . . the women more beautiful than flowers, more full of juice and succulence than fruit" (414). Similarly, when Wolfe views the city as an ocean, he treats the city's populace as so many tidal creatures, referring at one point to Abe Jones, the urbanite, as "a blind sea-crawl" (*OTR,* 468). Moreover, in the tradition of Wolfean ambivalence, his ocean-city either "invites all human drops of water to the grand oblivion of its ceaseless tides" (*WR,* 298), tides that are a "maelstrom of sound, movement, violence, and living tissue" (*OTR,* 423); or, more affirmatively, forms a living, mutual entity with its tidal inhabitants, an energy field within which people and buildings, the human ("breast") and the nonhuman ("stony"), seem to flow harmoniously in, around, and through each other:

> The city seemed carved out of a single rock, shaped to a single pattern, moving forever to a single harmony, a central all-inclusive energy—so that not only pavements, buildings, tunnels, streets, machines, and bridges, the whole terrific structure that was built upon its stony breast, seemed made from one essential substance, but the tidal swarms of people on its pavements were filled and made out of its single energy, moving to its one rhythm. He moved among the people like a swimmer riding the tide. (*WR,* 415)

Finally, Wolfe also brings nature into his texts through the use of his nature-based "wordscape" (Goldsmith, *The Modern American Urban Novel,* 15). In fact, nature serves as Wolfe's "master template," and, as a result, the earth provides for Wolfe, not only the ultimate reference point for the self, but also a universal, idiomatic "language" which serves as the ultimate lexicon for explicating life and all things in it. It appears, then, that he fully subscribed to Emerson's conception of the relationship between language and nature: "Words are signs of natural facts" ("Nature," 19). "We are," Emerson asserted, "assisted by natural objects in the expression of particular meanings" (23), and he thus emphasized that "the world is emblematic. Parts of speech are metaphors, because the whole of nature is a metaphor of the human mind" (23–24). A case in point is the section of Gant's dream in *Of Time and the River* where he leaves the road and enters a forest. From this point forward, the dream becomes a nature-based allegory of the passage from life into death, with the forest's fading light serving as a metaphor for Gant's impending death:

> And then . . . it seemed to [Gant] that all of the bright green-gold around him in the wood grew dark and sombre, the path grew darker, and suddenly he was walking in a strange and gloomy forest, haunted by the strange and tragic light of dreams. . . . And suddenly [Gant] knew that he had taken the wrong path, that he was lost. And in his heart there was an immense and quiet sadness, and the dark light of the enormous wood was all around him; no birds sang. (260–61)

Wolfe's rhetorical mining of nature is especially well illustrated by his use of animal tropes in his characterizations. Thus, Aunt Louise is "like a rabbit trapped before the fierce yellow eye, the hypnotic stare of a crouching tiger" [her husband, Uncle Bascom] (*OTR*, 144–45); Eliza is "octopal" (335); Ben, lying on his deathbed, is "like some enormous insect on a naturalist's table" (*LHA*, 452); the draymen outside Gant's shop are "like heavy buzzing flies" (84); the faces of South Carolina policemen "had a look of . . . a fathomless and mindless animal good nature, and at the same time a fathomless and mindless animal cruelty" (369); Laura James's eyes are "cat-green" (*LHA*, 355); Eugene, riding the subway, "would pant and gasp for life like a fish out of water" (151) when the train entered the Central Station; Upshaw, the gulled spouse, is "this withered squirrel of a man" (490); and the athlete, Jim Randolph, has the "nervous grace of a thoroughbred animal" (*WR*, 170). Wolfe especially saw people as so many species of the bird family, with *Look Homeward, Angel* resembling an imagistic aviary. Thus, "Eliza watched [her boarders] with a falcon's eye for thefts" (*LHA*, 112); sensual Jewesses are described as "protesting with their hen-feathered cries" (*OTR*, 479); old men are likened to "crested cocks" (147); Eugene sits "solemn as an owl" (*OTR*, 151); Sylvia, Abe Jones's sister, "was a woman . . . of a dark and almost bird-like emaciation" (459); the black children who daily entertain George Webber on their bikes "came like ravens with a swallow-swoop" (*WR*, 69); the young thespians at Altamont's Shakespearean Festival "twittered with young bird-laughter" (*LHA*, 309); Jake Abramson "brooded above [Esther Jack] like a benevolent vulture" (*YCGHA*, 187); Irene Mallard dances with Eugene "with hands held up like wings" (*LHA*, 393); Stanley Ward, a co-worker of Uncle Bascom, carries himself like a "pouter pigeon" (*OTR*, 118); a bar-maid has the "witty visage of a parrot" (606); an inn-keeper is "wren-like" (809); Esther wakes up "as quick and sudden as a bird" (*YCGHA*, 12); Margaret Leonard has "brown eyes [which] darkened into black as if a bird had flown through them and left the shadow of its wings" (*LHA*, 178); the boarders at Dixieland "scattered away like sparrows" (358); Laura James is "bird-swift" (380); and Will Pentland gives "a birdlike nod and wink" (12).

Just as numerous are Wolfe's characterizations which draw on images from non-sentient nature.[7] Thus, Esther has "a mane of dark black hair which somehow contrived to give a cloudlike, wild, and stormy look to her whole head" (*WR*, 294), and "everything went whirling in her brain like blown leaves that scurry in the Park in old October" (634); Abe Jones is "an obscure and dreary chrysalis" (*LHA*, 468); the sexual longing of John Dorsey's sister, Amy, is conveyed by the phrase, "like a pool she was thirsty for lips" (185); Ben's hair "is crinkled and crisp as lettuce" (137), and he is described at one point as "[walking] along . . . looking like asphodel" (423); people on a station platform have "white empetalled faces" (*OTR*, 25); two Filipinos in Pennsylvania Station are described as being "brown as berries" (*YCGHA*, 45); street urchins are seen as "[springing] up like dragon seed from the grim pavements of New York" (51); Eugene's face "was a dark pool in which every pebble of thought and feeling left its circle" (*LHA*, 101), and he "saw, from sea-sunk eyes, the town [of Altamont]" in the early morning; Laura "was a virgin, crisp like celery" (363), and "her hair fell down about her like thick corn-silk" (369); and Eugene's building superintendent has a "small parsley face" (*OTR*, 448). In addition, both human-made and organic objects are described, at times, in nonhuman terms. Thus, French taxis travel "with wasp-like speed" (*OTR*, 684), and the brain is figured as "a frightful bird whose beak was in [Eugene's] heart" (*LHA*, 186).

Wolfe also draws on the concrete, living metaphors of nature to frame abstractions, such as characterizing "facts" as being "bright as herrings in a shining water" (*OTR*, 422); capturing a boy's inchoate apprehension of some "vast pervasive presence" (*HD*, 78) in the night by asking, "Is it a lion in the mouth sulfurous, a fox in the eye humorous, a cat in the paw felonious, that prowls and breathes and stirs around night's great wall forever and that will not let us sleep?" (77); and by figuring the world encroaching on Altamont as "a kissing tide, which swings lazily in with a slapping glut of waters, and recoils into its parent crescent strength, to be thrown farther inward once again" (*LHA*, 111). This nature-izing of abstractions is especially well illustrated by his various conceptualizations of life and human existence. Thus, he refers to "the sea of life" (*WR*, 250), "the troubling weathers of a man's soul" (250), "this howling wilderness of life" (*YCGHA*, 27) and, in the specific cases of Eliza, Eugene, and George Webber, a "life Sargassic" (*LHA*, 240), a life "like a great wave breaking in the lonely sea" (426), and a life "buffeted in a mad devil's dance like a bird hurled seaward on the wind" (*WR*, 554), respectively. Wolfe also asserts that "all of our lives is written in the twisting of a leaf upon a bough, a door that opened, and a stone" (*OTR*, 155); that "human nature is, alas, a muddy pool, too full of sediment, too murky with the deposits of time, too churned up by unchartered currents in the depths and on the surface" (*YCGHA*, 561); and that "man's true home, beyond the ominous and cloud-engulfed horizon of the here and now, [lies] in the green and hopeful and still-virgin meadows of the future" (543).

Wolfe's methods for bringing nature "into" his texts are, therefore, versatile and wide-ranging, reflecting the unrelenting force and presence of his eco-consciousness. To the end, he remained a conduit for nature—for its wildness within himself and the nature-borne wildness he experienced all around him. Thus, for Wolfe, to write about cities, people, and ideas was necessarily to invoke nature because everything is, he felt, interrelated, organically derivable, and connected to the earth. Therefore, it is fitting that nature has the last word at the end of his tetralogy, that the earth, rivers, and winds which stir Eugene's eco-consciousness in *Look Homeward, Angel* are invoked in the last passage of the last section (Book VII: "A Wind is Rising, and the Rivers Flow") of his last novel:

> Something has spoken to me in the night, burning the tapers of the waning year; something has spoken in the night, and told me I shall die, I know not where. Saying:
>
> "To lose the earth you know, for greater knowing; to lose the life you have, for greater life; to leave the friends you loved, for greater loving; to find a land more kind than home, more large than earth——
>
> "——Whereon the pillars of this earth are founded, toward which the conscience of the world is tending—a wind is rising, and the rivers flow." (*YCGHA*, 576)[8]

Chapter Five

Look Homeward, Angel

Introduction to a Greener Modernism

While all of Wolfe's novels are permeated by nature's presence to varying degrees, *Look Homeward, Angel* is the greenest of them all, featuring the most integrated interaction between the natural world, the characters, and the story line. As a result, the organic world in *Look Homeward, Angel* is more integrally involved in the life and actions of the main protagonist than in any other of Wolfe's novels, an impression fostered by the novel's being set almost entirely in a rural setting, by the fact that Eugene assimilates his environment with the hypervigilance of a young Wordsworth, and by the fact that the pervasive encroachment of the natural world in *Look Homeward, Angel* is so palpable that it is as if the text were unable to resist the pressure of the organic world—such as when a breeze seems to waft, incongruously, through a classroom:

> They were to write a paper on the meaning of a French picture called The Song of the Lark. . . . Finally, the room was silent save for a minute scratching on paper.
>
> The warm wind spouted about the eaves; the grasses bent, whistling gently.
>
> Eugene wrote: "The girl is hearing the song of the first lark." (172)

The "split-screen" effect of this placement of indoor and outdoor imagery suggests not only the independent presence of nature apart from human will and consciousness, but also, given the textual contiguity of these images, the closeness that exists between human and nonhuman life, a closeness that is more pronounced in *Look Homeward, Angel* than in any other of Wolfe's novels. As a result, it is sometimes difficult to know where nature leaves off and a character's psyche begins. Thus, Eliza's ruminations about her unborn son, Eugene, become both textually embedded and imagistically immersed in autumn images: "And lying there while the winds of early autumn swept down from the Southern hills, filling the black air with dropping leaves, and making, in intermittent rushes, a remote sad thunder in great trees, she thought of the stranger who had come to live in her" (18).

While *Look Homeward, Angel* has been referred to as Wolfe's *Ulysses*, reflecting its modernist structural features, it could also be viewed as his "Prelude."[1] Here, Wolfe's consciousness of nature finds its most lyrical and emotion-laden expression, recalling Wordsworth's delight in the natural wonders of his Vale as recollected in the early chapters of "The Prelude" (1850). Given that Wolfe wrote *Look Homeward, Angel* in his twenties, when the memories of his hillbound life were still vivid and he was still imbued with a young man's ardor, and given that his reconstructed images draw on his former preternatural ability as a child to completely immerse himself in the objects of the human and nonhuman worlds, that is, when, like Eugene Gant, he saw the world "with the fresh washed eyes of a child, with glory, with enchantment" (*LHA*, 125), his representations of the natural world also reflect the most sustained freshness, intensity, and vivacity among his four novels. Since *Look Homeward, Angel* represents the "original ground" of his nature ideology, it makes sense that while the other novels also contain luminous nature passages, their reworked literary soil is unable to yield the vigor and bulk of Wolfe's first harvest of nature images. Not coincidentally, Wolfe's apprentice novel is also his most unambiguously romantic work of fiction and, concomitantly, his most elegant and passionate "protest" against modernist literature's cult of restraint. Thus, despite Wolfe's naturalistic reference to the earth as "this most weary and unbright cinder" in the proem, this novel offers Wolfean nature dressed in its most romantic and beneficent colors. Wolfe came to realize, however, as Wordsworth did, that it becomes more and more difficult to recover and recreate the joy and wonder we felt as children in our interactions with the natural world.[2]

If *Look Homeward, Angel* represents the originary expression of Wolfe's nature consciousness, then Gant's passage through the mountains into Altamont, which opens the novel, may be seen as the official entry into the natural "amphitheater" of Wolfe's fiction, a nature-ful setting whose ruling presence is invoked by the narrator's whimsical comment on the multi-tiered staging of the town's Shakespearean Festival:

> The town, in its first white shirting of Spring, sat on the turfy banks, and looked down gravely upon the bosky little comedy of errors; the

encircling mountains, and the gods thereon, looked down upon the slightly larger theatre of the town; and figuratively, from mountains that looked down on mountains, the last stronghold of philosophy, the author of this chronicle looked down on everything. (311)

Here, in the fictional World According to Wolfe, he, as director, authorizes the surrounding green world to play the role of Presiding Presence in the real-life dramas of the town.

Moreover, as this bildungsroman unfolds—the chronicle of a young man who is raised in a small town, feels alienated from his family, and begins to move out into the world beyond the protective ring of mountains, driven to find himself and the "lost lane-end into heaven" (proem)— it becomes clear that the text of Eugene's life would be unthinkable without being organically bound with the subtext of the natural world. In fact, *Look Homeward, Angel* represents the literary crucible of Wolfe's vision of what constitutes a life-defining relationship with the natural world. While nature plays a multitude of narrative and textual roles throughout Wolfe's fiction in the lives of his protagonists, its primary role in the life of the original Eugene Gant is that of a refuge—for imagination, feelings, companionship, comfort, contemplation, nurturance, (re)vitalization, solitude, protection, and healing. However, while Eugene uses nature to escape from the tumult of his family, as well as other pressures, he does not end up using it to escape from life; rather, his contact with the nonhuman world puts him back in touch with his own saving passion for living. Thus, his frequent engagement with nature also ensures that his lapses into modernist alienation and emotional numbness are not protracted. As the "still point" in his otherwise disruptive life, a life whose story incorporates modernist themes and issues, nature offers him a "way home," a means of finding his bearings, whenever he feels "lost."[3]

In only the third paragraph of *Look Homeward, Angel*, we are introduced to the notion that human affairs and nature are entangled in a world of chance: "The seed of our destruction will blossom in the desert, the alexin of our cure grows by a mountain rock, and our lives are haunted by a Georgia slattern, because a London cutpurse went unhung" (3). As if to dramatize this interconnectedness between the human and the nonhuman, the first chapter introduces Oliver Gant by playing him off against the landscape and the weather. In the process, an emotional profile emerges:

All day, under a wet gray sky of October, Oliver rode westward across the mighty state. As he stared mournfully out the window at the great raw land so sparsely tilled by the futile and occasional little farms, which seemed to have made only grubbing patches in the wilderness, his heart went cold and leaden in him. He thought of the great barns of Pennsylvania, the ripe bending of golden grain, the plenty, the order, the clean thrift of the people. (6)

Wolfe's treatment of Gant in this opening chapter foreshadows the extent to which he will draw on the natural world to narrate the text of *Look Homeward, Angel* and to construct its characters. Thus, for instance, Gant's heartsick view of the barren lowlands foreshadows his son's own emotional susceptibility to nature, and his spiritual attachment to the bountiful fields of Pennsylvania foreshadows Eugene's spiritual bond with the mountains and hills surrounding Altamont. In fact, Gant may be seen as not only the father of Eugene's nature consciousness, but also the father of nature's presence in Wolfe's fiction.

In hoping to escape his scandalous past and rebuild his life, Gant instinctively goes West, the Thoreauvian direction of wildness: "He turned westward toward the great fortress of the hills, knowing that behind them his evil fame would not be known, and hoping that he might find in them isolation, a new life, and recovered health" (5).[4] Gant's migration to the mountains sets the stage for Eugene's own discovery that the natural world is always "out there," always a potential refuge. As the narrator continues to chronicle the weather and the landscape outside Gant's train window, we see how the topography of his natural surroundings becomes progressively more West-like, more wild:[5]

Dusk came. The huge bulk of the hills was foggily emergent. . . . The train crawled dizzily across high trestles spanning ghostly hawsers of water. Far up, far down, plumed with wisps of smoke, toy cabins stuck to bank and gulch and hillside. The train toiled sinuously up among gouged red cuts with slow labor. (6)

After feeling disconsolate for most of the journey, Gant feels braced by the mountain weather:

As the horse strained slowly up the mountain road, Oliver's spirit lifted a little. It was a gray-golden day in late October, bright and windy. There

was a sharp bite and sparkle in the mountain air. . . . The trees rose gaunt
and stark: they were almost leafless. The sky was full of windy white rags
of cloud. (6–7)

Finally, upon seeing his new town for the first time, laid out on a plateau
and sheltered by hills, he greets it as his Promised Land:

> Then the sweating team lipped the gulch of the mountain, and, among
> soaring and lordly ranges that melted away in purple mist, they began
> the slow ascent toward the high plateau on which the town of Altamont
> was built.
>
> In the haunting eternity of these mountains, rimmed in their enor-
> mous cup, he found sprawled out on its hundred hills and hollows a
> town of four thousand people.
>
> There were new lands. His heart lifted. (7)

Tellingly, the uprooted Gant arrives in the fall, the season of letting go. He
then hibernates for the winter ("Oliver felt that he was crawling, like a
great beast, into the circle of those enormous hills to die" [6]) and, subsequently, is reawakened to life by the signs of spring: "And then the marvellous hill Spring came, green-golden, with brief spurting winds, the
magic and fragrance of the blossoms, warm gusts of balsam. The great
wound in Oliver began to heal" (8). Here, Gant demonstrates, as Eugene
will demonstrate later, that he resonates not only to the surface vibrations
of the earth, but to its inner (seasonal) rhythms as well. In fact, Gant's consciousness seems, at times, to inhabit the human and nonhuman worlds
simultaneously, a capacity that is poignantly illustrated when he meets the
Pentlands (his future wife's family) to the sound of windy rushes outside:
"And as they sat there in the hot little room with its warm odor of mel-
lowing apples, the vast winds howled down from the hills, there was a
roaring in the pines, remote and demented, the bare boughs clashed" (13).
As Gant listens, dividedly, to both the Pentlands and the wind, he confounds the wind's "remote and demented" sounds with the Pentland's
drawling talk of death and his own renewed feelings of loneliness and
despair: "And as their talk wore on, and Gant heard the spectre moan of
the wind, he was entombed in loss and darkness, and his soul plunged in
the pit of night, for he saw that he must die a stranger—that all, all but
these triumphant Pentlands, who banqueted on death—must die" (13).

Thus, while Gant's bond with the natural world can be a source of spiritual sustenance and hope, it can be a source of angst as well. Eugene will experience this same capacity of nature to elicit the full range of human emotions, such as when he comes to associate springtime with sadness as well as joy. When Ben asks Eugene if he has gotten over the loss of his first love, Laura James, with whom he had spent an enchanted spring the previous year, Wolfe writes:

> "No," said Eugene. In a moment he added: "She's kept coming back all Spring."
> He twisted his throat with a wild cry. (424)

Eugene's first contact with the earth is with Gant himself, a character best described in the idioms of nature. Wolfe initially figures him as a river, filling his home with the rich sediment of his life:

> His life was like that river, rich with its own deposited and onward-borne agglutinations, fecund with its sedimental accretions, filled exhaustlessly by life in order to be more richly itself, and this life, with the great purpose of a river, he emptied now into the harbor of his house, the sufficient haven of himself. (65)

As nature personified, Gant not only cultivates the vegetables and fruit trees of his Woodson Street lot, but also imparts to them a miraculous ripeness and fecundity:

> All that he touched waxed in rich pungent life: his Spring gardens, wrought in the black wet earth below the fruit trees, flourished in huge crinkled lettuces that wrenched cleanly from the loamy soil with small black clots stuck to their crisp stocks; fat red radishes; heavy tomatoes. The rich plums lay bursted on the grass; his huge cherry trees oozed with heavy gum jewels; his apple trees bent with thick green clusters. (55)

Given his persona as a green Prospero, Gant fittingly builds a house which is enclosed by honeysuckle ("The honeysuckle dropped its heavy mass upon the fence" [14]) and embowered by vines:

> His grape vines thickened into brawny ropes of brown and coiled down the high wire fences of his lot, and hung in a dense fabric, upon trellises, roping his domain twice around. They climbed the porch end of the house and framed the upper windows in thick bowers. (14)

Thus, while Gant feels cast out from his Pennsylvania Eden, he fathers his own homegrown Paradise, and it is within its protective green bowers that Eugene first becomes conscious of the world "out there." Moreover, Gant's house is Eugene's first nature-based refuge ("harbor," "haven").

Eliza, Eugene's mother, also has a green thumb, but she is a distracted Prospero: "her vegetables . . . flourished, as did all the earth, under her careless touch" (244). Moreover, while Gant's relationship with the earth is figured as personal and sensuous, Eliza's is figured as impersonal and economic: "Eliza saw Altamont not as so many hills, buildings, people: she saw it in the pattern of a gigantic blueprint. She knew the history of every piece of valuable property—who bought it, who sold it, who owned it in 1893, and what it was now worth" (104). Whereas Gant and the Eliza character in "The Web of Earth" are spiritually attached to the earth, the Eliza of *Look Homeward, Angel* is spiritually alienated. This disparity between Gant's and Eliza's closeness to the earth is symbolized by the fact that while Gant's house is firmly and snugly planted on the ground, Eliza's boarding house, the Dixieland, "its back end . . . built high off the ground on wet columns of rotting brick" (105), is precariously separated from the earth and vulnerable to windy drafts from below: "In winter, the wind blew blasts under the skirts of Dixieland" (104). While Woodson Street's warmth reflects Gant's nature-enriched spirit, Dixieland's coldness reflects Eliza's nature-impoverished persona. As a result, when Eliza takes seven-year-old Eugene to live with her at Dixieland, Eugene feels uprooted from fertile ground and transplanted to a relative wasteland. Not surprisingly, he seeks refuge at Woodson Street whenever possible:

> But the powerful charm of Gant's house, of its tacked and added whimsey, its male smell, its girdling vines, its great gummed trees, its roaring internal seclusiveness, . . . the comfort and abundance, seduced him easily away from the great chill tomb of Dixieland. (108)

As an infant, Eugene's first glimmerings of nature are gleaned from the sensory world all around him, a world that "swam in and out of his mind like a tide, now printing its whole sharp picture for an instant, again ebbing out dimly and sleepily, while he pieced the puzzle of sensation together bit by bit" (31–32). As time passes, some of these experiential fragments become attached, curiously, to the nonhuman world ("He was conscious of sunlight, rain, the leaping fire, his crib, the grim jail of winter"

[34]), and he begins to intuit that the outdoors, "out there"—where the weather comes from—can be a wondrous place, thus "hearing . . . the elfin clucking of the sun-warm hens, somewhere beyond in a distant and enchanted world" (32). After being first exposed to this world of sunlight and rain from his safe perch on the front porch, he is introduced further into this enchanted region when Gant, as nature's emissary, takes him from his basket and places him in a lily bed in the back of the lot, "under trees singing with hidden birds" (32). Eugene's sensory awareness is immediately drawn to the earth smells ("against the high wire fence there was the heavy smell of dockweed" [32]), and, during a subsequent backyard vigil, interacts with nature for the first time by imitating the "moo" of Swain's cow next door. Soon after, "loose . . . in the limitless meadows of sensations" (66), he penetrates even further into this outdoor world when he escapes from the yard by squirming underneath the back wire fence, thus proving his Gantian pedigree by instinctively "lighting out for the territory." A few years later, Eugene will share his father's passionate attentiveness to natural surroundings on a trip they take together to Augusta, Georgia: "The inner excitement of both was intense; the hot wait at the sleepy junction of Spartanburg, . . . the hot baked autumnal land, rolling piedmont and pine woods, every detail of the landscape they drank in with thirsty adventurous eyes" (125).

As Eugene matures, the world evolves from sensory chaos to sensual feast: "he felt the infinite depth and width of the golden world in the brief seductions of a thousand multiplex and mixed mysterious odors and sensations, weaving, with a blinding interplay and aural explosions, one into the other" (68–69). Moreover, the sensations of the green world draw his attention as much as the human world and, gradually, he begins to attach feelings to his nature-induced sensations: "Spring was full of cool dewy mornings, spurting winds, and storms of intoxicating blossoms, and in this enchantment Eugene first felt the mixed lonely ache and promise of the seasons" (55). This passage from sensory to sensual awareness is marked, textually, by an extended lyrical catalogue of felt experiences:

> He had felt now the nostalgic thrill of dew-wet mornings in Spring, the cherry scent, the cool clarion earth, the wet loaminess of the garden. . . .
>
> Yes, and the rank slow river, and of tomatoes rotten on the vine; the smell of rain-wet plums and boiling quinces; of rotten lily-pads; and of foul weeds rotting in green march scum; and the exquisite smell of the

South, clean and funky, like a big woman; of soaking trees and the earth after heavy rain. (69)

Eugene's sensual orientation to the green world is also decidedly Gantian rather than Pentlandian. Thus, while Eugene relishes the moneyed harvest he gleans when he peddles fruits and vegetables throughout the neighborhood, he does not associate this windfall with Eliza's sober notions of the earth's economic value, but with Gant's romantic notions of the earth's opulence: "he liked the work, the smell of gardens, of fresh wet vegetables; he loved the romantic structure of the earth which filled his pocket with chinking coins" (95). Eugene is not only close to the earth ("midget-near the live pelt of the earth" [71]), but also of the earth, as Wolfe notes how "he had grown up like a weed" (197), that "a strange wild thing bloomed darkly in his face" (197), and that he harbored a latent "Northern desire, a desire for the dark, the storm, the winds that roar across the earth" (125). Not surprisingly, this "wild child" first begins to apprehend the world on nature's terms: "he saw his life down the solemn vista of a forest aisle" (31).

Up to this point, Eugene has been drawn to the nonhuman world as a source of pleasure and fascination rather than as a medium of escape, the one exception being his periodic retreats to the greener pastures of Woodson Street. In fact, Eugene first comes to understand the escapist potential of nature through his imagination, an imagination first stirred by his avid reading of anything that invokes a marvelous world far, far from Altamont:

Thus, pent in his dark soul, Eugene sat brooding on the fire-lit book, a stranger in a noisy inn. The gates of his life were closing him in from their [his family's] knowledge, a vast aerial world was erecting its fuming and insubstantial fabric. He steeped his soul in streaming imagery, rifling the book-shelves for pictures and finding there such treasures as *With Stanley in Africa.* (68)

It does not take long, however, for Eugene to apply his bookish fantasies to a green world that is, for him, already enchanting. For example, in identifying with nature, he imagines that he is a demon wind: "he . . . sloped over singing pines upon a huddled town, and carried its guarded fires against its own roofs, swerving and pouncing with his haltered storm upon their doomed and flanking walls, . . . calling down the bullet-wind" (74). It is the sight of the surrounding hills and mountains, however, that becomes for him his most compelling avenue for imaginative escape:

"Beyond the hills the land bayed out to other hills, to golden cities, to rich meadows, to deep forests, to the sea. Forever and forever" (160); "The world was a phantasmal land of faery beyond the misted hem of the hills, a land of great reverberations, of genii-guarded orchards, wine-dark seas, chasmed and fantastical cities" (89). In fact, at this stage Eugene treats *all* mountains as gateways to escapist landscapes: "Thus, lost in the remote Ozarks, he wandered up Central Avenue, fringed on both sides by the swift-sloping hills, for him, by the borders of enchantment, the immediate portals of a land of timeless and never-ending faery" (132).⁶ Rivers are equally capable of transporting him to faraway places. Thus, on one of his trips into the South with Eliza, he imagines the Mississippi as lapping exotic shores: "he looked upon the huge yellow snake of the river, dreaming of its distant shores, the myriad estuaries lush with tropical growth that fed it, all the romantic life of plantation and canefields that fed it" (129). Such fantasies enable Eugene to escape not only "the grimy smudges of life" (89), but also the pall of Eliza's pedestrian outlook: "So did his boundaries stretch into enchantment—into fabulous and solitary wonder broken only by Eliza's stingy practicality, by her lack of magnificence in a magnificent world" (128).

As Eugene matures, his treatment of nature as a fantasy kingdom will wane, and his erstwhile child's window on the world will be supplanted by an emerging romantic outlook. In chronicling this shift in perception at the end of the novel, Wolfe notes, "It was not his quality as a romantic to escape out of life, but into it. He wanted no land of Make-believe; his fantasies found extension in reality" (491). In effect, Eugene's innate appreciation for the unembellished grandeur of the natural world—its wondrous ordinariness—ends up demystifying any would-be visions of big rock candy mountains:

> The commonness of all things in the earth he remembered with a strange familiarity—he dreamed of the quiet roads, the moonlit woodlands, and he thought some day he would come to them on foot, and find them there unchanged, in all the wonder of recognition. They had existed for him anciently and forever. (134)

While nature will continue to stir his imagination, it will no longer be a source of unreality but, rather, reality itself, drawing him back to his senses. Accordingly, whereas the mountains surrounding Altamont had initially taken him out of the world, they now become for him "the cup of reality, beyond growth. . . . They were his absolute unity in the midst of eternal change" (158).

Nature "as it is" also offers him companionship. While Ben has his dark angel to commune with, Eugene has all the earth, a felt kinship that has a tonic effect on him. Thus, during his secret and solitary dialogues with the nonhuman world, his emotional self, otherwise buried inside, feels summoned from its hibernation: "As that Spring ripened he felt entirely, for the first time, the full delight of loneliness. Sheeted in his thin nightgown, he stood in darkness by the orchard window of the back room at Gant's, drinking the sweet air down, exulting in his isolation in darkness" (167); "In winter, he went down joyously into the dark howling wind, leaning his weight upon its advancing wall as it swept up a hill; and when in early Spring the small cold rain fell from the reeking sky he was content. He was alone" (249). This communion with the nonhuman world also emboldens him to unabashedly sound out his paean to life, to loose his animal spirits: "As the wind yelled through the dark, he burst into maniacal laughter. He leaped high into the air with a scream of insane exultancy, burred in his throat idiot animal-squeals. . . . He was free. He was alone" (250). Ultimately, Eugene so completely identifies his loneliness with nature that, at Norfolk, Virginia, he apostrophizes the sea as his own, lonely doppelganger: "O sea, I am lonely like you" (436).

Given that Eugene seems to thrive best under the protective aegis and nurturing presence of the nonhuman world, it is fitting that he should first envision his "spiritual mother" (192), school teacher Margaret Leonard, as a "great pool of dawn" that bathes him in "the white core and essence of immutable brightness" (178). It is also fitting that he should find her amid a pastoral setting: "He liked to be there [the Altamont Fitting School] most in the afternoons when the crowd of boys had gone, and when he was free to wander about the old house, under the singing majesty of great trees, exultant in the proud solitude of the fine hill, the clean windy rain of acorns, the tang of burning leaves" (192). Within this nature-blessed sanctuary, Margaret acts as mother bird to Eugene's fledgling and vulnerable self; she "nested his hooded houseless soul" (179). When he leaves her nest, Eugene will go to yet another pastoral shelter, that of the state university at Pulpit Hill, located incongruously amid bland tobacco lands:

> The countryside was raw, powerful and ugly, a rolling land of field, wood, and hollow; but the university itself was buried in a pastoral wilderness, on a long tabling butte, which rose steeply above the country. . . . The central campus sloped back and up over a broad area of rich turf, groved with magnificent ancient trees. . . . There was still a good flavor of the wilderness about the place—one felt its remoteness, its isolated charm. It seemed to Eugene like a provincial outpost of Rome: the wilderness crept up to it like a beast. (329)

While the school's "wilderness" is conflated in Eugene's mind with seclusion and beauty, its backwoodsy-ness seems ill-suited to a place of cultural uplift: "He read Poe's stories, *Frankenstein*, and the plays of Lord Dunsany. . . . Then for the first time, he thought of the lonely earth he dwelt on. Suddenly, it was strange to him that he should read Euripides there in the wilderness" (351–52). Yet, in fact, Eugene ends up viewing Pulpit Hill as a cultural clearing. At the same time, it is, in the tradition of Greek pastoral, more a place for satyrs to gambol than for young men to study, an environmental phenomenon that is especially manifest in the springtime, when "the rare romantic quality of the atmosphere, the prodigal opulence of Springtime, thick with flowers and drenched in a fragrant warmth of green shimmering light, quenched pretty thoroughly any incipient rash of bookishness" (330). The greening magic of spring is somehow magnified here, and, as evidence, Eugene's common "animal-squeals" (250) become mythologized as "the centaur-cry of man or beast" (348). When, after four years, he finally leaves the campus, his passage back to the prosaic world will be marked, both literally and metaphorically, by his descent from "that Arcadian wilderness where he had known so much joy" (503) to the "hot parched countryside below" (504).

In coming out of this wilderness, Eugene brings with him, paradoxically, more worldly wisdom. In the tradition of Faulkner's Ike McCaslin ("The Bear"), Eugene loses his innocence and finds enlightenment in the woods. In fact, the signs of Eugene's more mature outlook had already become evident on his trips home, when, for the first time, he began to see his familiar hills as smaller than he remembered. Thus, upon returning to Altamont after his first term at Pulpit Hill, "his loins . . . black with vermin" (343) from having slept with a prostitute, his reaction to the town and hills is similar to Gant's on his return from California: "How looked the home-earth then to Gant the Far-Wanderer? . . . the hills were big, but nearer, nearer than he thought. . . . He stepped carefully down in squalid Toytown, noting that everything was low, near, and shrunken as he made his Gulliverian entry" (58). Eugene similarly sees the same town and hills as Lilliputian in scale: "The hills, above the station flats, with their cheap propped houses, had the unnatural closeness of a vision . . . it was as if he devoured toy-town distances with a giant's stride" (343). Later, when he returns home for his second Christmas while at college, still wounded by Laura's desertion, he "found the hills bleak and close, and the town mean and cramped in the grim stinginess of winter" (407). While Gant measures the mountains against the broader scale of the West, Eugene now measures them against his more expansive window on life. When "the mountains were his masters" (158), the center of his world, he lacked both spatial and worldly perspective. Now, there are moments when the mountains seem to have been reduced to comparative objects in a world whose center is indeterminate.

Despite Eugene's more chastened vision of life, he nevertheless continues to find comfort in the natural world, even in the same downsized hills. Thus, before reaching Altamont on the same return from college when he was disease-ridden, "[his] sick heart lifted in the eternity of the hills" (343). Similarly, it is only after he walks in the same hills that he decides to get help from his brother, Ben. In fact, in seeming alliance with nature, Eugene experiences the clearing of his own mental and spiritual fog while witnessing the sun clearing the mist below, the "still point" of nature here serving to both ease his fretfulness and "illuminate" his vision:

> He walked with aimless desperation, unable to quiet for a moment his restless limbs. He went up on the eastern hills that rose behind Nigger-town. A winter's sun labored through the mist. Low on the meadows, and high on the hills, the sunlight lay on the earth like milk.
>
> He stood looking. A shaft of hope cut through the blackness of his spirit. I will go to my brother, he thought. (344)

He is again uplifted by the surrounding hills when he returns home that summer and recoils from the welter of war activity ("Eugene came up into the hills again and found them in their rich young summer glory" [355]); and, later that same summer, Eugene and Laura James seek solace in their "timeless valley," the most memorable instance in the text of nature's sheltering beneficence. Here, surfeited by a crossfire of elemental sights, sounds, and smells, the lovers are able to temporarily leave behind the unkind "practical" world: "Laura and Eugene lay upon their backs, looking up through the high green shimmer of leaves at the Caribbean sky, with all its fleet of cloudy ships. The water of the brook made a noise like silence. The town behind the hill lay in another unthinkable world. They forgot its pain and conflict" (377). As a prelude to this epiphanic moment, Eugene had noticed en route to the valley that whereas the town seemed chaotic, the hills embodied orderliness:

> There seemed to be a kind of centre at the Square, where all the cars crawled in and waited, yet there was no purpose anywhere.
> But the hills were lordly, with a plan. (375)

In fact, Eugene feels more than just cut off from the human world "down there"; more accurately, he feels *joined* in "a single passionate lyrical noise" (378) to this "other" world of "flower and field and sky and hill, and all the sweet woodland cries, sound and sight and odor" (378). Inspired by the felt security of these hills, Eugene asks Laura to secret herself in the mountains while waiting for him to return from fabled travels: "I am going all over the world. I shall go away for years at a time. . . . You shall live in a house away in the mountains, you shall wait for me, and keep yourself for me" (363).

As Eugene's fellow pilgrim on their flight into the hills, Laura also succeeds Margaret Leonard in playing Mother Earth to Eugene's motherless life: "She saw his hand, wrapped in its bloody bandage: she nursed it gently with soft little cries of tenderness" (363). Unfortunately, Laura's proffered sanctuary is not as "timeless" as their valley, proving to be, as she is, more mythical and evanescent than real and lasting. Thus, while she embodies nature ("she had the firm young line of Spring, budding, slender, virginal" [356]), she ends up offering Eugene only a glimpse of Arcadia rather than the solid earth: "She was like something swift, with wings, which hovers in a wood—among the feathery trees suspected, but uncaught, unseen" (356–57). In a poignant rite of passage, Eugene learns that nature, no matter how romanticized, can also be indifferent.

When Laura withdraws her "shelter," Eugene seeks consolation and comfort in the primal mothering of Mother Nature herself. After reading

Laura's farewell letter, he walks up into the hills and, as darkness descends, feels cleansed by the star-struck night: "It was night, vast brooding night, the mother of loneliness, that washes our stains away. He was washed in the great river of night, in the Ganges tides of redemption. His bitter wound was for the moment healed in him: he turned his face upward to the proud and tender stars" (382).[7] Later, still wounded by his loss of Laura, he resolves to spend the summer working in the war industry at Norfolk, where, upon arrival, he immediately feels his life resuscitated by the sea:

> Within a few minutes he had left the hot murky smell of the shed and was cruising out into the blue water of the Roads. A great light wind swept over the water, making a singing noise through the tackle of the little boat, making a music and glory in his heart. . . . The lean destroy-ers . . . and the light winey sparkle of the waves fused to a single radiance and filled him with glory. He cried back into the throat of the enormous wind, and his eyes were wet. (426)

Later, standing on one of the beaches, he experiences how the sea's lyrical and transcendent voice is able to harmonize not only the seaport's carni-val clatter at his back, but also his own internal cacophony; in the process, he feels his loneliness beautified: "And that cheap music turned elfin and lovely; it was mixed into magic—it became a part of the romantic and lovely Virginias, of the surge of the sea, as it rolled in from the eternal dark, across the beach, and of his own magnificent sorrow" (436). Nature also serves as a healing agent immediately after Ben dies, when Luke and Eugene find refuge from death in the waking sounds of nonhuman (and human) life as they walk to town. During this scene, a cock crows, after which Wolfe, referring to Eugene's own thoughts, writes, "But the cock that crows at morning (he thought), has a voice as shrill as any fife. It says, we are done with sleep. We are done with death. O waken, waken into life" (468). Later, Eugene again experiences nature's healing grace when he returns to Ben's cemetery plot. After being serenaded by a medley of stars, wind, and leaves, which draws his attention to the continuous, "deathless" presence of organic life all around him, Eugene is soothed by the knowl-edge that Ben will return "in flower and leaf" (486). When he returns to Pulpit Hill that spring, the greening of the earth further assuages his grief until, finally, the earth recycles his sorrow back into new life: "He was wild with ecstasy because the Spring had beaten death. The grief of Ben sank to a forgotten depth in him. He was charged with the juice of life and motion" (587).

In effect, nature provides the stable nurturance and anchoring that Eugene never receives at Dixieland, and he thus emerges at the end of the novel a more fully developed person than he would have been otherwise. He is also bolstered by the knowledge that nature will always "be there" for him: "But, amid the fumbling march of races to extinction, the giant rhythms of the earth remained. The seasons passed in their majestic processionals, and germinal Spring returned forever on the land—new crops, new men, new harvests, and new gods" (519). He is, in fact, ready to find himself, to begin in earnest "the last voyage, the longest, the best" (521); and he knows that he must go both inland (within himself) and beyond the shelter of the familiar hills. It is, therefore, fitting that while the novel begins with Gant's passage into the mountains, the novel ends with Eugene's visionary passage beyond them:

> Yet, as he stood for the last time by the angels of his father's porch, it seemed as if the Square already were far and lost; or, I should say, he was like a man who stands upon a hill above the town he has left, yet does not say 'the town is near,' but turns his eyes upon the distant soaring ranges. (522)

In seeking to find himself, Eugene, still fluent in the idioms of nature, first vows, "I will plumb seas stranger than those haunted by the Albatross" (521). Ultimately, he envisions his quest as a wilderness journey, identifying his self as an elusive satyr-like being lost within the wilds of his mind and body: "O sudden and impalpable faun, lost in the thickets of myself, I will hunt you down until you cease to haunt my eyes with hunger" (521). In order to capture and reclaim the faun, Eugene must first create a sunlit clearing within himself. This accomplished, he will no longer need the surrogate parenting of nature: he will finally be able to put down his own roots and know where he stands.

Chapter Six

The Miraculous Spring

Passion and Nature Redeem the Wasteland

Although *Look Homeward, Angel* represents Wolfe's most romantic depiction of nature, his romantic outlook remains the most unifying element of his treatment of nature throughout his oeuvre. Thus, cataloguing Wolfe's greening methods and perceptions of nature risks giving the impression that his approach is the sum of disparate but related elements when, in fact, the romantic aspects of his treatment of the natural world constitute a coherent body of beliefs that organize his greening methods within a holistic frame. Moreover, it is Wolfe's romanticism that most succinctly accounts for the ideological and rhetorical differences between his handling of the nonhuman world and that of his contemporaries. It also explains why his unrestrained style should not be viewed simply as the outpourings of an undisciplined writer; there is, it turns out, an organic, nature-based method to his prose.

While the romantic strains in Wolfe's style have been amply documented, there has been little ecocritical interest in the romantic reverberations in his treatment of the natural world.[1] Rather, the focus has been on the romantic nature of Wolfe's language and beliefs, the influences of specific romantic poets, and Wolfe's qualifications as a romantic character.[2] Moreover, just as the critics have been more interested in the figurative, rather than literal, implications of the romantics' "nature writing," so Wolfe's critics have been more interested in his thematic use of nature than his view of the natural world.[3]

In fact, both Wolfe and the romantics could not conceive of humankind apart from the nonhuman world. Karl Kroeber argues that the romantics were "proto-ecological" in their handling of nature, a term which "is meant to evoke an intellectual position that accepts as entirely real a natural environment existent outside one's personal psyche" (*Ecological,* 19). Based on this orientation, the romantics "believed that humankind *belonged* in, could and should be at home within, the world of natural processes" (5).[4] Wolfe's fiction is similarly dependent on his characters being situated within the natural world. Thus, to talk about Wolfe's romanticism is not just to categorize his style, but also to characterize his approach to nature.

Wolfe's and the romantics' apprehension and representation of nature is the product of an individualized, interrelational, subjective, sensual, and emotional process of experience. Their nature images are "created" through the interactive, ecological relationship between an individual's mind (imagination) and the natural world, a dynamic eloquently illustrated in Wordsworth's treatment of "the infant Babe" (237) in Book II of "The Prelude": "Along his infant veins are interfused / The gravitation and the filial bond / Of nature, that connect him with the world" (262–64), "From nature largely he receives; nor so / Is satisfied, but largely gives again" (267–68), "his mind, / Creates, creator and receiver both, / Working but in alliance with the works [of nature] / Which it beholds" (271–75). In Wordsworth's "Home at Grasmere," he calls for, in M. H. Abrams' words, a "holy marriage" (31) between the mind and nature, a marriage which will imaginatively remake the world, and he bases his faith in such a union on the organic "fit" between the mind and nature:

> How exquisitely the individual Mind
> (And the progressive powers no less
> Of the whole species) to the external world
> Is fitted; and how exquisitely, too—
> Theme this but little heard of among men—
> The external world is fitted to the mind;
> And the creation (by no lower name
> Can it be called) which they with blended might
> Accomplish: this is my great argument.
> (1006–1014)

Implicit in this celebration of the "fit" between human consciousness and the "external world," and of nature's creative partnership ("blended might") with humankind, is the romantics' conception, shared by Wolfe, of the evocative presence of the nonhuman world, "this *active* universe" ("The Prelude," Book II, 266), in human lives. This is exemplified by Wordsworth's practice of using active, transitive verbs to characterize nature's impact on human consciousness: "Ye mountains! thine, O Nature! Thou hast fed / My lofty speculations" ("The Prelude," Book II, 462–63); "The sounding cataract / Haunted me like a passion" ("Tintern Abbey," 77–78). Wolfe and the romantics especially valued nature's fundamental stimulus to the imagination. At the same time, both also believed that while the imagination is capable of transfiguring the same physical world that evokes its power, the ordinary earth *is*, by its very nature, an enchanted place. Wolfe invokes this credo in his observation of Eugene's Gant's changing outlook on life:

> And as all the strength and passion of his life turned more and more away from its childhood thoughts of aerial flight and escape into some magic and unvisited domain, it seemed to him that the magic and unvisited domain was the earth itself, and all the life around him—that he must escape not out of life but into it. (*OTR*, 389)

In experiencing this same philosophical shift in outlook, George Webber discovers that his imagination becomes no less enchanted by being anchored to the earth:

> His was increasingly the type of imagination which gains in strength as it grows older because it is rooted to the earth. It was not that since his childhood he had grown disillusioned, nor that the aerial and enchanted visions of his youth had been rubbed out by the world's coarse thumb. It was now just that Pegasus no longer seemed to him to be as interesting an animal as Man-O'-War—and a railroad roundhouse was more wonderful to him than both of them. (*WR*, 316)

Inspired by the wonder of actual horses and railroad roundhouses, Wolfe would, as Wordsworth did, "throw over them a certain colouring of imagination, whereby ordinary things should be presented to the mind in an unusual way" ("Preface to *Lyrical Ballads*," 597). Thus, in *Look Homeward, Angel*, the narrator plays up the extraordinariness of ordinary dandelions: "The grass was thick with dandelions: their poignant and wordless odor studded the earth with yellow magic. They were like gnomes and elves, and tiny witchcraft in flower and acorn" (377). In fact, Wolfe was able, as were Wordsworth, Melville, and Thoreau, to traffic effortlessly between concrete observations and figurative impressions of the same natural phenomena.

The romantics not only viewed nature as a wellspring for the imagination, but also as the organic fuel for human vitality and the engines of life.

As Jonathan Bate has pointed out, "Wordsworth wrote poems about how flowers may vitalize the human spirit" (39). Not surprisingly, then, the romantics celebrated life's inherent and ineluctable movement in all its guises and forms.[6] Wolfe expresses this vitalistic concept in the section of *Antaeus, or A Memory of Earth* where the wife of Furman, her home having just been destroyed in a flood, yearns for an existence apart from all rivers, change, and movement: "O God! Just let me live where nothin' moves! Just let me live where things will always be the same!" (71). Nature's movement and changes, however, are inescapable, and Wolfe underscores this universal and organic reality when Furman's wife realizes that her consciousness continues to be lapped by the rivers of life:

> I know each sound that's comin' from the River! I hear the willows trailin' in the River! I hear the oak-limbs snagged there in the River! All my thoughts are flowin' like the River, all of my life is movin' like the River, I think an' talk an' dream just like the River, as it flows by me, by me, to the sea. (72)[7]

Based on their notion that nature acts as a vitalizing agent, with the senses serving as the conduit, the romantics valued emotions not only because they are individualistic and subjective responses, but also because they are the signs and expressions of vitality. According to Kroeber, "Wordsworth treats emotions as the psychic manipulation of sensation, the process by which psychic activity, inner impulse, mingles and coordinates with physical sensation, the reception of stimuli from outside" (*Romantic Landscape Vision*, 35). Wolfe's writing suggests that he shared this same belief in the external, sensory-drawn origin of human emotions. Based on this belief, the romantics valued pleasurable feelings the most and "joy" in particular.[8] Wolfe himself speaks reverently of joy: "when a person has in him the vitality of joy, it is not a meaningless extravagance to say that 'nothing else matters.' He is rich. It is probably the richest resource of the spirit" (*WR*, 353). The romantics viewed joy as not only being "at its highest . . . the sign in our consciousness of the free play of all our vital powers" (Abrams, 433), but also, according to Coleridge, as the pathway to a state of oneness with the physical world. In the case of Coleridge's poem, "Dejection" (1802), M. H. Abrams points out that "joy . . . is described as the inner power which unites the living self to a living outer world" (277), a world which is, itself, characterized by organic unity.

Thus, to participate in any organic, interactive process was, for both Wolfe and the romantics, necessarily to form a joyous communion with the *unity* of life.[9] Moreover, the romantics "regarded natural processes as being *intrinsically* joyous" (Kroeber, *Ecological,* 43), an attitude that is manifest in Eugene Gant's joyful response to the sensory influx of the nonhuman world: "Suddenly spring came, and he felt at once exultant certainty and joy" (*OTR,* 137).

Not only do emotions tap, express, and reflect the organic vitality of nature, but they also "color" perceptions of it as well. Thus, the landscape *is* what it *feels* like to the observer at the moment of perception or retrospection.[10] Although this mutability of perception and "reality" invites ambivalence—because neither the emotions nor the landscape holds still—the romantics treated this phenomenon as a cause for celebration because it indicates the lively pageant and lability of human emotions in interplay with the ongoing, variable conditions of the earth.[11] Wolfe's changing and contradictory perceptions of *all* landscapes are in this same spirit of perceptual and emotional immediacy and, as with the romantics, he celebrated light and dark nature scenes with equal passion in his texts. Thus, Wolfe writes in *The Web and the Rock* that "the mountains in Wintertime had a stern and demonic quality of savage joy that was, in its own way, as strangely, wildly haunting as all of the magic and the gold of April" (151). As indicated by this reference to the mountains' "quality of savage joy," the externalization of feelings onto the physical world also meant that the phenomena of nature were treated as sentient; and, in fact, one of the trademarks of Wolfe's treatment of the natural world is his pervasive use of personification: "The wind howled through the rocking trees with insane laughter" (*YCGHA,* 458). Moreover, unlike the romantics, Wolfe treated the human-made world as sentient as well: "The house became like a living presence. Every object seemed to have an animate vitality of its own—walls, rooms, chairs, tables, even a half-wet bath towel" (10).

The romantics also "tended to regard thoughts as constituted of emotions" (Kroeber, *Ecological,* 5) and deliberately sought to induce their readers to *feel* the world. This promotion of human feelings reflected, in part, their principled stand on the limited capacity of scientific rationalism to make sense of the external world. Although they valued the scientific study of natural phenomena and believed that by studying the various parts of nature, science "could on occasion provide a means of increasing our ability to learn from, and more efficaciously interact with, the natural world" (16), they concurrently believed that science was incapable of capturing the essence, or wholeness, of nature. Rather, the meaning of the natural world could best be apprehended from a subjective, imaginative perspective which was colored by feelings. This was Wolfe's stance and method as well.

Wolfe also shared the romantics' notion that nature embodies beneficent qualities that may be tapped by human beings with open senses. Specifically, nature may be imbibed as a salutary force, a healing balm, and a source of spiritual and physical renewal, qualities which are especially manifest in springtime. Even a businessman such as Mr. Jack, who inhabits a world of denatured habitats, is susceptible to the palliative powers of the earth: "The smell of earth which he [Mr. Jack] had caught in the air this morning was good, and the remembrance of it laid a soothing unction on his soul" (YCGHA, 125). In also sharing the romantics' belief that nature emblematizes the great truths of life, Wolfe saw eternity embodied in the mountains, life and time embodied in the Hudson, and human mortality embodied in the browning leaves of October. For both Wolfe and the romantics, nature also instills spiritual feelings, a secular faith in the natural processes all around them.[12] Thus, in Look Homeward, Angel, the narrator expresses sentiments similar to those contained in Wordsworth's reference to "that spirit of religious love in which / I walked with Nature" ("The Prelude," Book II, 377–78) when he likens a hillside forest to "a vast green church" (376), and later asks, "Who walks with us on the hills?" (179–80).

To a great extent, then, Wolfe's writing style is the organic and rhetorical outgrowth of his ideology of nature and his artistic negotiation between the human and the nonhuman.[13] In fact, in recalling his experience in Of Time and the River, he figures it as a "flood tide chaos of creation" (SN, 38), during which he "had inside, swelling and gathering all the time, a huge black cloud, and . . . this cloud was loaded with electricity, pregnant, crested, with a kind of hurricane violence that could not be held in check much longer" (37). Subsequently, "the storm did break," and he became overwhelmed by a "torrential and ungovernable flood" of words; and "upon that flood everything was swept and borne along as by a great river. And [he] was borne along with it" (37).[14] Thus, he notes elsewhere "that every man on earth held in the tenement of his flesh and spirit the whole ocean of human life and time, and that he must drown in this ocean unless, somehow, he 'got it out of him'" (*WR*, 248).

Although the romantic strains in Wolfe's writing had become less frequent and florid by the time of his death, partially in deference to his critics and partially as the waning of a young man's idealistic ardor, his eco-consciousness continued no less to color his writings. Thus, one of the last fictional texts he was working on, "The Hills Beyond," while considered by Aswell "without a doubt his most objective work" (301), nonetheless represents a spiritual return to his native earth and is arguably as much about the land and the characters' relationships to it as about the characters' relationships with each other. Moreover, his last nonfictional work, the travelogue that was to be published as *A Western Journal*, features all the old hallmarks of Wolfe's romantic sensibilities; as he surveyed and recorded the West of the late 1930s, he reclaimed and reasserted his Wordsworthian rhetoric, inviting the landscape to inscribe itself on his senses, emotions, and imagination. Thus, regardless of the ebb and flow of his romantic aesthetics, his romantic view of nature—whose core ecological tenet is humankind's existence within the organic nexus of life—continued to be a vital and guiding force in his writing and thinking up until his death.

Wolfe's texts were not, of course, the only ones in the 1920s and 1930s to situate stories within nature, to convey a deep valuation of the earth, or to dramatize how people can establish strong attachments to the land. However, there are substantive differences in how Wolfe and his contemporaries *figure* nature in their texts, and much of these differences can be attributed to Wolfe's romantic ideology. While the treatment of nature in the fiction of the 1920s and 1930s contained, in general, only vestiges of romantic thinking and leitmotifs (such as the pathetic fallacy), Wolfe's romantic treatment was pronounced. As a result, Wolfe produced a different rendering of nature and contact with the nonhuman world at a time when romantic sentiments and style in literature were viewed pejoratively as evidence of lingering genteelness. He especially adhered to the romantic tradition of treating the apprehension of nature as a subjective, sensual, and emotional process, and his representations of the nonhuman world reflect this orientation. Thus, he figured nature as a landscape of feelings and sense-impressions and, as a result, treated the natural world with greater emotional range, intensity, and engagement than did his contemporaries in fiction and poetry. In Wolfe's fictional world, emotional contact is as palpable and compelling as any physical contact.

For the purposes of comparison, Hemingway may be seen as Wolfe's opposite in style. Most noticeably, Hemingway's taciturnity and indirectness juxtaposes to Wolfe's verbosity and directness. Hemingway pared all inessential words from his text, leaving only the figurative tip of the iceberg, a tip which was meant to resonate with deep meaning, even deep emotion. According to his "iceberg theory," the art of writing was showing rather than telling; it was the power of suggestion. As such, emotions were to be conveyed, as was everything else, by "understatement and indirection" (Love, "*The Professor's House,*" 298). At its best, Hemingway's relatively terse, unembellished prose produces "charged spareness" (295) and "understated intensity" (307) in its representation of experience. By comparison, Wolfe's writing draws its overstated intensity and emotional surcharge from its verbiage and its wrought and evocative language. In a letter to F. Scott Fitzgerald in July of 1937, Wolfe counters Fitzgerald's charge that his writing is not selective enough—and, by implication, suffers from rhetorical excess—by noting that "every novel, of course, is a novel of selected incidents. There are no novels of unselected incidents" (*LTW,* 643). He goes on to point out that his style of selectivity also places him in a grand tradition of literary composition:

> Well, don't forget, Scott, that a great writer is not only a leaver-outer but also a putter-inner, and that Shakespeare and Cervantes and Dostoievsky were great putter-inners—greater putter-inners, in fact, than taker-outers—and will be remembered for what they put in—remembered, I venture to say, as long as Monsieur Flaubert will be remembered for what he left out. (643)

Hemingway himself grumbled about Wolfe's copious style. In a letter to Charles Scribner (February 24, 1940), he expressed his resentment over what he perceived as Maxwell Perkins's misplaced interest in Wolfe by writing, "Why can't he take an interest in me like he took in Tom? I will let him cut out useless bits of what I write if that is what he likes" (*Selected Letters,* 503). Aside from Wolfe's rhetorical opulence and Hemingway's niggardliness, their stylistic differences are further accentuated by their subjective and objective points of view, respectively. As a result, not only is their writing radically different, but so, too, are their renderings of nature; in fact, they seem to be apprehending a different nature altogether. Thus, in Hemingway's painstakingly objective description of trees in the following passage from *In Our Time,* any latent vitality is understated through his use of spartan language, static images, and detached tone:

> There was no underbrush in the island of pines. The trunks of the trees went straight up or slanted toward each other. The trunks were straight and brown without branches. The branches were high above. Some interlocked to make a solid shadow on the brown forest floor. Around the grove of trees was a bare space. ("Big Two-Hearted River," 183)

By comparison, Wolfe's subjective representation of a plum tree in *Look Homeward, Angel*—wordier, more descriptive, more figurative, and more evocative—appears vital and alive:

> in the Spring, lithe and heavy, she will bend under her great load of fruit and blossoms. . . . Red plums will ripen. . . . They will fall bursted on the loamy warm wet earth; when the wind blows in the orchard the air will be filled with dropping plums; the night will be filled with the sound of their dropping, and a great tree of birds will sing, burgeoning, blossoming richly, filling the air also with warm-throated plum-dropping bird-notes. (137)

Wolfe's transfiguring images of ripeness and pleasing sounds also "dress" his tree in a celebratory mood, and, in fact, while Hemingway's tone in figuring nature is generally constant and low-keyed, Wolfe's tends to be variable and high pitched. In Hemingway's case, his indiscriminately low pitch of excitement acts as an emotional depressant, tending to mitigate the degree of felt engagement between his characters and their surroundings. Thus, while his sensory references serve as a linguistic bridge to the environment, they do not necessarily convey a sense of emotional closeness with it. In *The Sun Also Rises* (1926), Jake's low-keyed manner treats the landscape as an unfolding mural which needs to be reported rather than as something to engage with emotionally. Similarly, while there is much visual engagement with the terrain in *Green Hills of Africa* (1935), it is conveyed with little emotion; the hunter-narrator must keep his cool, and he responds to the nature all around him with similar cool. This emotional detachment creates a "gap" between the perceived environment and the actual, felt environment.

Moreover, while Hemingway will occasionally comment directly on his characters' feelings, his more characteristic method is to convey feelings through "silences" which are "filled in" by the reader. The result of this suggestive style, however, is that the identity of the characters' feelings is often rendered indeterminate. Moreover, even when Hemingway comments directly on a character's feelings, as when he says in "Big Two-Hearted River" that "[Nick] was happy" (179), the overall flattened tone of the prose tends to drain such overt emotional expressions of any depth; it is just another objective observation in a series of objective observations: "Nick walked back up the ties to where his pack lay in the cinders beside the railway track. He was happy. He adjusted the pack harness around the bundle" (179). Still, there are critics who feel that the very covertness of Hemingway's expressive style yields emotional dividends; that he artfully uses flatness, paradoxically, to conjure what otherwise would remain latent emotion. Nevertheless, the specific emotional overlay of a passage, or a character's specific emotion, still remains difficult to decipher. By contrast, Wolfe more overtly indicates not only the type of emotions his protagonists are experiencing in the presence of nature, but also nature's evocative role in the emotion-making process: "The air was filled with dropping leaves, there was a solemn thunder of great trees upon the hills; sad phantasmal whisperings and the vast cathedral music deepened in his heart" (LHA, 249). Here, Eugene's sensations of sadness are clearly evoked by the trees' "music." Thus, not only do Wolfe's characters appear to respond more emotionally to the nonhuman world than Hemingway's, but his natural landscapes appear to be more "emotionalized" as well.

The same issues concerning the emotional presence and resonance of nature passages come up in comparisons between Wolfe and Willa Cather. Given that Cather espoused and practiced a theory of writing which closely resembles Hemingway's iceberg theory, her treatment of nature is ostensibly closer to Hemingway's than to Wolfe's.[15] However, while most critics view Cather's "unfurnished" prose as having the same "hidden" capacity as Hemingway's to stir strong emotional reactions in the reader, Cather is less spare than Hemingway and arguably more imaginative and descriptive. In addition, while her expression of emotion is generally covert, her texts nonetheless contain selective nature passages which are lucidly descriptive and imbued with overt expressions of feeling. One such scene is Tom Outland's epiphanic experience atop the mesa in "Tom Outland's Story" (Book Two, *The Professor's House* [1925]): "And the air, my God, what air!—Soft, tingling, gold, hot with an edge of chill on it, full of the smell of pinions—it was like breathing the sun, breathing the color of the sky" (*Five Stories*, 61).[16] Cather is also willing at times to "tell" rather than dramatize her characters' feelings— thus, Tom Outland recalls, "For me the mesa was no longer an adventure, but a religious emotion" (68)— and to use figurative language to dramatize the landscape's capacity to stir the imagination: "but the mesa top would be red with sunrise,—metallic, like tarnished gold-foil" (26); "Then the mesa was like one great ink-black rock against a sky of fire" (26); "The arc of sky over the canyon was silvery blue, with its pale yellow moon, and presently stars shivered into it, like crystals dropped into perfectly clear water" (68). Similarly rich, figurative descriptions can also be found in the narrator's recordings of the landscape in *Death Comes to the Archbishop* (1926): "The wind was like a hurricane at sea, and the air became blind with snow" (126); "in the west, behind the mountain, lay a great stationary black cloud, opaque and motionless as a ledge of rock" (119). Overall, however, while Cather and Wolfe are both invested in conveying impressions of the nonhuman world, and while both attach feelings to such impressions, Wolfe's descriptions of nature are geared, as Cather's are not, to conveying the immediacy of nature-induced emotions and contact with nature in general. Compare, for example, their different handling of scenes which depict a character's letting-go to the organic world. In the following passage from *My Ántonia* (1918), Jim Burden recalls having lain in his grandparents' garden:

> The earth was warm under me, and warm as I crumbled it through my fingers. . . . I was something that lay under the sun and felt it, like the pumpkins, and did not want to be anything more. I was entirely happy. . . . At any rate, that is happiness; to be dissolved into something complete and great. (14)

While Jim describes the scene by utilizing sensual ("crumbled," "felt") and figurative ("I was something that lay under the sun") language, and even an overt declaration of feeling ("that is happiness"), he communicates his *experience* by talking about his feelings ("that is happiness") rather than feeling them directly; in effect, his ever-present ego-consciousness ("I") ends up intellectualizing his experience and mitigating the emotional depth and immediacy of his felt responses and, consequently, also mitigates the felt closeness between Jim and the natural world.[17] In a comparable scene, Wolfe describes Eugene Gant as immediately experiencing his feelings about the natural world rather than thinking about them, thus closing the experiential gap between himself and nature. Thus, as Eugene is exposed to a spring landscape whose figurative topography resembles a veritable minefield of metaphors and similes—"The day was like gold and sapphires: there was a swift flash and sparkle, intangible and multifarious, like sunlight on roughened water, all over the land. A rich warm wind was blowing, turning all the leaves back the same way, and making mellow music through the lute-strings of flower and grass and fruit" (*LHA*, 376)— he is depicted as not only immersed in nature, but also emotionally overwhelmed by it: "The boy grew blind with love and desire: the cup of his heart was glutted with all this wonder. It overcame and weakened him" (376). The evocative puissance of this green world, as measured by its figurative depth, invades Eugene's senses and wrings all feeling from his body, and, as a result, the human/nonhuman boundaries seem to break down. While Jim Burden's ego-consciousness remains noisily present, Eugene's ego-consciousness is rendered mute, overwhelmed by a cataract of nature-induced feelings and sensations. Thus, as a result of Cather's and Wolfe's rhetorical differences in representing their scenes, Wolfe's description of Eugene's contact with the physical world appears more immediate, felt, and engaged than Burden's.

John Steinbeck's *The Grapes of Wrath* (1939) offers another useful comparison with Wolfe's emotion-based treatment of nature. This story of the Joads' displacement and subsequent wandering in a post-Depression landscape begins by chronicling the evolution of the Dust Bowl conditions and, in doing so, establishing the impression that the ensuing action is by characters whose lives are ultimately framed and governed by nature. While this contextualizing of the narrative within the organic world is similar to Wolfe's orientation, the impoverished emotional contact between Steinbeck's characters and the land is not. Having been both traumatized and disoriented by their uprooting, the characters are psychologically disconnected from their originary touchstone, the earth, and their newly adopted "anchor" becomes the open road:

> They were not farm men any more, but migrant men. And the thought, the planning, the long staring silence that had gone out to the field, went now to the roads, to the distance, to the West. That man whose mind had been bound with acres lived with narrow concrete miles. And his thought and his worry were not any more with rainfall, with wind and dust, with the thrust of crops. Eyes watched the tires, ears listened to the clattering motors. (268)

This impression of separation from the land, which manifests in the characters' emotionally flat responses to their surroundings, is reinforced by the fact that, first, the characters direct very few comments toward their natural surroundings;[18] second, due to Steinbeck's objective point of view, when the narrator observes and describes the landscape, we generally have no way of knowing whether the characters are experiencing the same phenomena; and, finally, whereas in the interchapters the migrants' emotional responses to the land are addressed directly, in the regular text the Joads' emotional responses to the land are conveyed indirectly, that is, based primarily on no other evidence than their words and narrative context.[19] Moreover, when the Joads do talk about the changing landscape, their comments seem either perfunctory or emotionally ambiguous. For example, when upon first catching sight of California, Tom Joad says, "This here's a murder country. This here's the bones of a country" (178); while he appears surprised and sobered by the starkness of the terrain, there is no indication that he's experiencing disappointment, anger, or some other emotion. What, if any, feeling has the landscape elicited from him? By contrast, there is usually no such ambiguity in the reactions of Wolfe's protagonists, as Wolfe transparently links their emotions to the evocative impact of the landscape. In the following passage from *Of Time and the River,* the coloring and intensity of Eugene's feelings are clearly drawn from the ambiance of his surroundings:

> And it was all so wonderful—the sleeping woods, the moon-enchanted fields, the slow, light grazings of the moonlit cows, and all the fragrance of the night, the grass, the clover and the meadow spells, and the magic warmth and loveliness of the girl, and her sweet, low voice beside him in the moonlight—that it seemed to him that all his life had been a prelude and a preparation to this wonder. He did not know what he could say, it came swelling up, in a wild flood of tenderness and passion. (527)

The upshot of this ecological exchange between feelings and landscape, between the human and the nonhuman, is that "the moon-enchanted fields" and the "magic warmth" of the girl seem to cast a mutual spell over each other in Eugene's consciousness.

Finally, it is instructive to compare Wolfe's handling of nature with that of the South's most celebrated writer, William Faulkner, as he may be seen as the closest in style to Wolfe among the fiction writers of his time; and, in fact, the differences between them are more of degree than kind. For example, not only is Faulkner's fiction typically southern in featuring the compelling presence of nature, but many of his descriptions of the organic world are equally as romantic and poetic as Wolfe's. Faulkner also presents subjective impressions of nature through his characters, even sometimes outdoing Wolfe's own subjectivism by using first person points of view. Thus, Quentin's reconstructed perceptions and sensations in *The Sound and the Fury* (1929): "I could smell the curves of the river beyond the dusk and I saw the last light supine and tranquil upon tideflats like pieces of broken mirror, then beyond them lights began in the pale clear air, trembling a little like butterflies hovering a long way off" (195). The primary reason Faulkner was not himself criticized for being a retrograde romanticist is because he was *recognized* as a modernist and, as such, his romantic passages were seen as studied efforts to fractionate his rhetoric as well as his structure. Since Wolfe has historically not been viewed as a "legitimate" modernist, his romantic writing has been dismissed as merely regressive; whereas Faulkner was granted poetic license to diversify his language, Wolfe was not. While their similarities are great, what most differentiates them is the relative loudness of the emotional voices they use to vocalize their romantic, rich, and sensual descriptions of nature: while Wolfe's rhetoric is typically set at a high volume, Faulkner's descriptions come across more as soft-spoken, devotional musings. In addition, given that Faulkner's typical characters are not aesthetes, as Wolfe's are, they are not as well equipped, linguistically, to appreciate nature's beauty and, accordingly, they generally don't apprehend nature in romantic terms; rather, this is left to the narrator. Thus, whereas Faulkner's treatment of the Quentin character in *The Sound and the Fury* is an exception to this rule, his handling of the Quentin character in *Absalom, Absalom!* (1936) is more representative. In this case, romantic observations are superimposed on, rather than originating from, the character: "he *seemed* [emphasis mine] to feel the dust itself move sluggish and dry across his sweating flesh just as he seemed to hear the single profound suspiration of the parched earth's agony rising toward the imponderable and aloof stars" (362). Thus, while Faukner's characters notice the natural world, they rarely do so or are described as doing so with any great passion. In sound-making terms, whereas Faulkner's descriptions of the green world are more characteristically sonorous, Wolfe's are more characteristically lyrical, drawing on rising and falling emotional decibels that personalize the environment and, as a result, draw nature closer into meaningful contact.

Therefore, what most distinguishes Wolfe's treatment of nature from that of his contemporaries in fiction is the heightened level of contact he achieves through his use of emotion and, Faulkner excepted, a subjective perspective, a methodology that draws on both nature's capacity to evoke feelings and humankind's capacity to be emotionally receptive to non-human phenomena. This romantic, emotion-based handling of nature distinguishes his treatment of the natural world from that of his contemporaries in poetry as well.

Viewing Wolfe's treatment of nature in the context of the poetry of the 1920s and 1930s makes sense if for no other reason than to compare T. S. Eliot's handling of the nonhuman world with Wolfe's. In fact, Wolfe's treatment of nature is both an affirmation of his own romantic ideology and a repudiation of the modernists' wastelander ideology as embodied in Eliot's verses. In Eliot's "The Waste Land" (1922), the narrator's emotional withdrawal from springtime is, if anything, an anti-romantic gesture and, in fact, Wolfe counters Eliot's "April is the cruellest month" passage with his affirmative comments on spring throughout his work, with the following passage appearing as a direct rejoinder to Eliot's poem by ironically invoking the word "cruellest" in a paean to spring:

> What things will come again? O Spring, the cruellest and fairest of the seasons, will come again. And the strange and buried men will come again, in flower and leaf the strange and buried men will come again, and death and dust will never come again, for death and the dust will die. (*LHA*, 486)[20]

The last section of "The Waste Land"—"What the Thunder Said"— describes a barren, rocky land unrelieved by any greenery or hope: "Here is no water but only rock / Rock and no water and the sandy road / The road winding above among the mountains / Which are mountains of rock without water" (331–34). Here, in language that is as emotionally barren as the landscape, Eliot depicts nature as oppressive, antagonistic, and inhospitable to humankind and, consequently, his characters' lives appear impoverished. By comparison, Wolfe, in *Of Time and the River,* not only counters this image when he asks if human passion and vitality have not thrived in the American landscape, but also challenges the ethos of the "old men," such as Eliot, who have forgotten how to live, who have "poured into our hands a handful of dry dust and ashes" (148):

> The dry bones, the bitter dust? The living wilderness, the silent waste? The barren land?
>
> Have no lips trembled in the wilderness? No eyes sought seaward from the rock's sharp edge for men returning home? Has no pulse beat hot with love or hate upon the river's edge? Or where the old wheel and the rusted stock lie stogged in desert sand: by the horsehead a woman's skull. No love? . . . Was no love crying in the wilderness?
>
> It was not true. The lovers lay below the lilac bush; the laurel leaves were trembling in the wood. (149)

While Eliot himself was not, of course, a "nature poet," there were many poets during these two decades who appropriated nature's images to make meaning of both life and the times in which they lived. Specifically, they used nature, as Wolfe did, to ground their texts in what they viewed as the green world's steadfast integrity and its predictable and enduring presence amid widespread cultural instability. At the same time, while there were some poets who shared with Wolfe the same *idea* of nature, their handling of the nonhuman world was, compared to his, emotionally distant and constrained.

Like Wolfe, Robert Frost emphatically situates his narrators and characters within the natural world. Unlike Wolfe, however, his speakers tend to think nature rather than feel it. While Wolfe lets go to nature as an object for emotional assimilation, Frost lets in nature as an object for contemplation. In effect, Frost keeps his feet on the ground at all times. Based on this stolid stance, the emotional gradient of his verses tends to be restricted, narrowly, to a "light" or "dark" *mood,* and his measured lines, as well as his equable, conversational, and Yankee-flat delivery impose a brake on both emotional abandon and intensity. This being said, there are exceptions to this rule, poems which express, however tepidly, emotional resonances in response to nature. At the same time, the speakers in these poems typically *talk about*—rather than directly experience—their feelings, such as the speaker's claim to being a "slave to a springtime passion for the earth" (9) in "Putting in the Seed" (1916). Still, for every poem which enacts a relationship between nature and the speaker's feelings, there are far more which enact a relationship between nature and the speaker's thoughts. Thus, Frost's most characteristic poems are those which use nature or an object of nature to think their way through, in the form of self-conscious monologues, to some resolution which occurs in the form of an aphoristic insight. In "A Minor Bird" (1928), Frost has the speaker use the title bird to address his aversion to open expressions of joy. While the speaker begins the poem by stating, "I have wished a bird would fly away, / And not sing by my house all day" (1–2), he ends up by mildly reproving himself with the words, "And of course there must be something wrong / In wanting to silence any song" (7–8). In fact, Frost tended to "silence," or at least mute, his own singing voice. By comparison with Frost's more cerebral relationship to nature, Wolfe, in *The Web and the Rock,* has George Webber respond emotionally to snow that is, itself, emotionally drawn:

> Snow fell that night. It began at six o'clock. It came howling down across the hills. . . .
>
> George Webber went to sleep upon this mystery, lying in darkness, listening to that exultancy of storm, to that dumb wonder, that enormous and attentive quietness of snow, with something dark and jubilant in his soul he could not utter. (134)

The "exultancy of [the] storm" clearly elicits "something dark and jubilant" in George's soul.

If there is an emotional gap that distinguishes Wolfe's treatment of nature from Frost's, there is an emotional and methodological bridge between Wolfe and Hilda Doolittle. H. D. wrote poems that draw on nature's images with a Wolfean passion and intensity. However, H. D.'s passion is most often attached, in Imagist fashion, to objects rather than to the speaker. While she externalizes her emotions, as Wolfe does, often the exchange is one-way; the objects feel *for* the narrator and, as a result, any sense of an ecological exchange—and, concomitantly, an emotional closeness with nature—is vitiated. In "Oread" (1915), for example, although

H. D.'s speaker characteristically invokes the quickening forces of wild nature, the speaker and nature remain separate; as a result, the splashing, hurling, and whirling of the sea—together with any attached emotion— remain apart and withheld from the poem's human presence:

> Whirl up, sea—
> whirl your pointed pines.
> splash your great pines
> on our rocks,
> hurl your green over us,
> cover us with your pools of fir.
> (*Collected Poems*)

When, however, nature-borne energy does manage to penetrate the body and consciousness of H. D.'s speaker, there is an emotional or physical reaction that is similar in intensity to what Wolfe's protagonists experience when sensually overloaded by their natural surroundings: "The light beats upon me. / I am startled— / a split leaf crackles on the paved floor— / I am anguished—defeated" ("Mid-Day," 1–4), "The heavy sea-mist stifles me. / I choke with each breath—" ("Loss," 6–7).[21] By the time of her 1931 publication of *Red Roses for Bronze*, however, many of her poems were deviating from her "spare, intense, and evocative" style (Quinn, *Hilda Doolittle* [*H. D.*], 91). As a result, her emotional treatment of nature grew more tame. Thus, in "Sea Choros (From Hecuba)," the heretofore unguarded feelings attached to nature are now tempered within the constraints of a dramatized and stylized rhetoric, language which serves to further increase the distance between the speaker and the nonhuman world:

> Wind of the sea,
> O where,
> where,
> where,
> through the salt and spray,
> do you bear me,
> in misery? (1–7)

By comparison, in the 1930s Wolfe was chanting his lyrical and passionate paean to October in *Of Time and the River* (1935).

While Marianne Moore shared Wolfe's view that nature is indifferent to human life, as enunciated in her 1924 poem, "A Grave" ("the sea has nothing to give but a well excavated grave" [line 6]), her nature language, unlike Wolfe's, can sound indifferent as well. Though her poetry characteristically exudes a sense of curiosity and wonder, and her tone can be whimsical, she tends to maintain a scholarly distance from her natural subjects, the so-called "real toads" of her "imaginary garden." In her many poems centered on a species of animal, her equable tone resembles the narrative voice-over of a documentary; what emotion is present is mostly conveyed through the ironic descriptions of her animal subjects in human terms. Thus, in "The Frigate Pelican" (1935), she writes,

> . . . . .This one
> finds sticks for the swan's-down dress
> of his child to rest upon and would
> not know Gretel from Hansel.
> As impassioned Handel—
>
> meant for a lawyer and a masculine German domestic
> career—clandestinely studied the harpsichord
> and never was known to have fallen in love,
> the unconfiding frigate bird hides
> in the height and in the majestic
> display of his art . . . . (22–32)

While such jesting reinforces her pose as a delighted observer of nature, the academic (even, at times, pedantic) tenor of her verses imposes an emotional matter-of-factness, an impression that is fostered, in "An Octopus" (1935), by her combined use of true-to-nature descriptions and borrowed quotations:

> "Picking periwinkles from the cracks"
> or killing prey with the concentric crushing rigour of the python,
> it hovers forward "spider fashion
> on its arms" misleading like lace;
> its "ghostly pallor changing
> to the green metallic tinge of an anemone-starred pool." (10–16)

While Moore was fascinated by the nuances of the animal kingdom, she seems to have sought only intellectual stimulation from her study of it; though there is an implied passion in her interest in nature, there is little passion in the rhetoric of her verse.

Like Wolfe, Robinson Jeffers revered all natural and wild things. In his poem, "Life from the Lifeless" (1933–35), he apostrophizes nature with unabashed awe: "But look how noble the world is. / The lonely-flowing waters, the secret- / Keeping stones, the flowing sky" (13–15). However, unlike Wolfe and the romantics, he was content to eliminate the human from his picture of nature altogether. Thus, in "The Place for No Story" (1930–31), he describes a particular wild region, "The coast hills at Souvranes Creek" (1), as "the noblest thing I have ever seen. No imaginable / Human presence here could do anything / But dilute the lonely self-watchful passion" (9–11). By contrast, not only could Wolfe and the romantics not conceive humankind without nature, but they also could not conceive nature without humankind. Colored by his cynical attitude toward humankind and "civilization," Jeffers's references to nature are characteristically somber and elegiac in tone; while his emotions are fervent, they are restricted to this one blue note. Thus, Wolfe's joyful noises would have seemed discordant, even vulgar, to Jeffers; nature was to be addressed, as indicated in "Self-Criticism in February" (1935–38), with a seriousness that reflected the saber-rattling portents in Europe, not celebrated with high, piping voices: "the present time is not pastoral, but founded / On violence, pointed for more massive violence" (7–8).

Aside from his romantic rhetoric and perspective, what is perhaps most "Wolfean" about Wolfe's approach to nature is a matter of degree—as befits a writer noted for his excesses. While other contemporary novelists and poets shared his valuation of nature, few drew attention in their texts to the emotional nature of human "contact" with the nonhuman world and, when they did, they fell far short of matching the intensity of feeling with which Wolfe's alter-egos encounter nature and are stirred by the exchange. As such, Wolfe's handling of nature contravened the modernist practice and credo of mistrusting strong displays of emotion. As a result of this emotional "gap," there were few nature-oriented texts written during Wolfe's literary career whose narrative voices could compare with the nature-induced euphoria of Eugene Gant ("In winter, he went down joyously into the dark howling wind" (LHA, 149) or the emotional persona of

Wolfe's natural world: "And above them the stormy wintry skies . . . bent over them forever with that same unutterable pain and sorrow, . . . that spirit of exultant joy, that was gleeful, mad, fierce, lonely" (*WR*, 152). If the literature of the 1920s and 1930s could be viewed as so many musical scores, then Wolfe may be seen as having "played" nature at a more emotionally intense, higher pitched, and variable key than his contemporaries. Moreover, this playing not only added vibrancy to his representations of nature, but also insinuated a more pronounced emotional chord into his protagonists' relationships with the nonhuman world. In feeling their surroundings so deeply, his protagonists' bonds with nature were also rendered closer and more intimate than those of most other characters and narrators who inhabited the same contemporary fictional landscape.

Wolfe's treatment suggests over and over again that the natural world can arouse the nature within us, evoking emotional responses that can be as uncontrollable as nature itself. It also suggests that a romantic response to nature, one that is personal and surcharged with emotion, can thrive in narratives that are set in a modernist world, thus challenging our view of modernist fiction as constituting, uniformly, a narrative space where strong feelings are exiled and emotional energy is measured, in Eliot's memorable phrase, "with coffee spoons" ("Prufrock," line 51). For Wolfe, any imagined wasteland can be undone if we are able to tap the source of our life and passion; if we hearken to the stirrings of the earth:

> "Lean down your ear upon the earth, and listen"
> —*You Can't Go Home Again,* 40

Notes

Chapter 1

1. See, for example, the lyricist and formalist reviews of *Look Homeward, Angel* by, respectively, Margaret Wallace, "A Novel of Provincial American Life," *New York Times Book Review,* 27 October 1929, 7, and W. E. H, "A Modern Epic of the Life of a Pennsylvania Youth," review of *Look Homeward, Angel,* by Thomas Wolfe, Boston Evening Transcript, 9 November 1929, 2.

2. See Claude Simpson, Review of *You Can't Go Home Again,* by Thomas Wolfe, *Southwest Review* 26 (1940): 132–35 and Joseph Henry Jackson, "The Last Work of Thomas Wolfe, Significant Artist of His Time," *San Francisco Chronicle,* 5 July 1939, 13.

3. *Look Homeward, Angel* (Reprint, New York: Charles Scribner's Sons, 1957), and *Of Time and the River* (New York: Charles Scribner's Sons, 1935), comprise the first two novels of Wolfe's tetralogy. The remaining texts are *The Web and the Rock* (Reprint, New York: Perennial Library, 1973), and *You Can't Go Home Again* (Reprint, New York: Perennial Library, 1989).

4. Kenneth Brown claims in 1984 to have noted a "weatherchange in Wolfe criticism" (46). He points to the increased volume and scope of scholarship being done on Wolfe, and adds that "a far greater portion of this material is analytical and scholarly than was true years ago, and thus by nature more sober and less personal, but even the straightforward criticisms seem to be more temperate and sympathetic" (46). At the same time, studies of Wolfe in major journals have been in relative decline in the 1980s and 1990s. According to John Bassett, writing in the mid-nineties, "In the last fifteen years there has been very little commentary at all in the major journals about Thomas Wolfe" John E. Bassett, *Thomas Wolfe: An Annotated Critical Bibliography* (Lanham, Md.: Scarecrow, 1986).

5. The "throwback" aspects of Wolfe's writing have not been perceived in a negative light by all critics. In fact, as John L. Idol Jr. has pointed out in *A Thomas Wolfe Companion* (Westport, Conn.: Greenwood, 1987), that many scholars have placed the nature and quality of Wolfe's prose in august company:

His critical defenders rallied to his cause by proclaiming his manner Rabelaisian, Elizabethan in its energy, flow, and daringness, Miltonic in its grandeur, Whitmanesque in its rhapsodic response to the American scene, Melvillean in its willingness to bend language to meet artistic needs, Biblical in its ability to catch the directness and rhythm of everyday speech, and DeQuinceyean in its handling of the contrapuntal effects of phrasing. (68)

6. Carol Ingalls Johnston notes in *Of Time and the Artist: Thomas Wolfe, His Novels, and the Critics* (Columbia, S.C.: Camden House, 1996), that "Wolfe's energies were pitted against the fashionable critical theorists of the twenties and thirties, Humanists and Agrarians, Marxists and Freudians, as much as they were pitted against the Genteel Tradition of the earlier century" (2). In referring specifically to Wolfe's verbosity, John L. Idol Jr. notes:

> The battle lines were clear here: the lovers of the opulent style had much to praise; devotees of the Attic style found much to damn. Had Wolfe not been writing in an age delighting in a parsimonious style, as exemplified by Hemingway, the battle lines would not have been so far-flung or so hotly contested. (*Companion,* 68)

7. See John L. Idol Jr., "Thomas Wolfe and T. S. Eliot: The Hippopotamus and the Old Possum," *Southern Literary Journal* 13, no. 2 (1981): 15–16.

8. Diana Orendi Hinze's essay, "William Faulkner and Thomas Wolfe," *Thomas Wolfe Review* 12, no. 1 (1988): 25–32, represents a rare instance where Wolfe is portrayed as influencing the modernist icon (Faulkner), and not the other way around.

9. In "Thomas Wolfe: The Escapes of Time and Memory," in *Epiphany in the Modern Novel* (Seattle: University of Washington Press, 1971), Morris Beja reviews the modernist use of epiphanic moments by Wolfe, Joyce, Woolf, and Faulkner. According to Beja, "Moments of revelation are probably more frequent in the works of Thomas Wolfe than in those of almost any other novelist" (148). For additional information on the topic of Wolfe and epiphany, see Maurice Natanson, "The Privileged Moment: A Study in the Rhetoric of Thomas Wolfe," *Quarterly Journal of Speech* 53 (1997): 143–50.

10. The most prominent studies of Wolfe's "sense of place" have focused on the city, the South, the mountain region of western North Carolina, and, to a lesser extent, home and America. For critical studies of Wolfe's treatment of the city, see Louis D. Rubin Jr., "The City," in *Thomas Wolfe: The Weather of His Youth* (Baton Rouge: Louisiana State University Press, 1955); Felice Witztum

Dickstein, "The Role of the City in the Works of Theodore Dreiser, Thomas Wolfe, James T. Farrell, and Saul Bellow" (Ph.D diss., City University of New York, 1973); Blanche Housman Gelfant, "The City as Symbol," in *The American City Novel* (Norman: University of Oklahoma Press, 1954): 119–32; Leslie Field, "*The Web and the Rock*: The City, Esther and Beyond," *Thomas Wolfe Review* 11, no. 1 (1987): 11–18; Thomas E. Boyle, "Frederick Jackson Turner and Thomas Wolfe: The Frontier as History and as Literature," *Western American Literature* 4 (1970): 273–85; Lawrence Clayton "An example of Ambiguous Imagery in *You Can't Go Home Again*," *Thomas Wolfe Review* 3, no. 1 (1979): 15–17; James D. Boyer, "The City in the Short Fiction of Thomas Wolfe," *Thomas Wolfe Review* 7, no. 2 (1983): 36–40. For critical studies of Wolfe's treatment of the South, see Hugh C. Holman, "The Web of the South," in *Loneliness at the Core* (Baton Rouge: Louisiana State University Press, 1975): 107–37; Paschal Reeves, "Thomas Wolfe and the Family of Earth," in *The Poetry of Community: Essays on the Southern Sensibility of History and Literature,* ed. Lewis P. Simpson (Atlanta: Georgia State University Press, 1972): 47–54; Anne Rowe, "Thomas Wolfe in New York," *Thomas Wolfe Review* 5, no. 1 (1981): 36–41; Floyd Watkins, "The Sum of All the Moments," in *Thomas Wolfe's Characters: Portraits from Life* (Norman: University of Oklahoma Press, 1957): 179–84; David Herbert Donald, "Look Homeward: Thomas Wolfe and the South," *Southern Review* 23 (1987): 241–55; Louis D. Rubin Jr., "Thomas Wolfe and the Place He Came From," *Virginia Quarterly Review* 52 (1976): 183–202. For critical studies of Wolfe's treatment of the mountain region of western North Carolina, see Elmo Howell, "Thomas Wolfe and the Sense of Place," *South Carolina Review* 11, no. 1 (1978): 96–106; Ruel E. Foster, "Thomas Wolfe: Mountain Gloom and Glory," *American Literature* 44 (1973): 638–47; James Meehan, "Thomas Wolfe as Regional Historian," *Thomas Wolfe Newsletter* 1, no. 1 (1977): 9–11; Shelby Stephenson, "Elements of Lyricism in *Look Homeward, Angel,*" *Thomas Wolfe Review* 20, no. 1 (1996): 79–86; Leslie Field, "*The Hills Beyond*: A Folk Novel of America," *New York Folklore Quarterly* 16 (1960): 203–15. For a critical study of Wolfe's sense of home, see Suzanne Stutman, "Home Again: Thomas Wolfe and Pennsylvania," *Resources for American Literary Study* 18, no. 1 (1992): 44–52. For critical studies of Wolfe's treatment of America, see Boyle, "Frederick Jackson Turner and Thomas Wolfe"; M. N. Smrchek, "*Of Time and the River*: Wolfe, Whitman, and America," *Thomas Wolfe Review* 9, no. 1 (1985): 24–30; Hugh C. Holman, "Thomas Wolfe and Amercia," *Southern Literary Journal* 10, no. 1 (1977): 56–74; Richard Walser, "America and Poetry," in *Thomas Wolfe: An Introduction and*

Interpretation (New York: Barnes & Noble, 1961): 1–11; Herbert J. Muller, "Wolfe and the Tradition," in *Thomas Wolfe* (Norfolk, Conn.: New Directions, 1947): 161–89. See also note 12 in this section for selective (eco)critical studies of Wolfe's treatment of nature.

11. Thus, for instance, Gelfant asserts in her preface to *The American City Novel* (1954), "I have avoided a geographical or topographical approach to urban life and fiction" (vii). In addition, the southern and "Appalachian" studies have been conducted, with few exceptions, in the context of the cultural rather than the physical landscape, and the studies of Wolfe's treatment of America as a place have been mostly concerned with aesthetic issues. Even Boyle's treatment of Wolfe's use of organic, western, and frontier images of the city is subsumed under his study of Wolfe's aesthetic struggle to reconcile the actual with the ideal in his writing.

12. For some notable exceptions to this standard critical approach to Wolfe and nature, see Foster; John Hagan, "The Whole Passionate Enigma of Life: Thomas Wolfe on Nature and the Youthful Quest," *Thomas Wolfe Review* 7, no. 1 (1983): 32–42; and Shawn Holliday, "The Pity, Terror, Strangeness, and Magnificence of It All: Landscape and Discourse in Thomas Wolfe's *A Western Journal*," *Thomas Wolfe Review* 21, no. 2 (1997): 34–45.

Chapter 2

1. Maxwell Perkins, in "Scribners and Thomas Wolfe," in *Always Yours, Max*, ed. Alice R. Cotton (Rocky Mount, N.C.: The Thomas Wolfe Society, 1997): 92–99, writes that it was Wolfe's acknowledgment and awareness of the distinctiveness of America's environment that challenged his ability to transcribe it into words:

> He knew that the light and color of America were different; that the smells and sounds, its peoples, and all the structures and dimensions of our continent were unlike anything before. It was with this that he was struggling, and it was that struggle alone that, in a large sense, governed all he did. (91)

2. See Richard Walser, "America and Poetry," in *Thomas Wolfe: An Introduction and Interpretation* (New York: Barnes & Noble, 1961): 1–11.

3. Wolfe tried to prove to his detractors that he could write more objectively and with greater structural control than he had in his first two novels. He was also motivated by the desire to have his short stories accepted for

magazine publication. Still, the vast majority of his oeuvre may be character-ized as variations on the same Wolfean style which enraptured the lyricists and offended the formalists.

4. In *The Window of Memory* (Chapel Hill: University of North Carolina Press, 1962), Richard Kennedy suggests that Wolfe's style owes as much to his own personal vitality as to any philosophical influence such as vitalism: "the enormous gusto in his psalm of life reflects his own vitality as much as it does any theory of Life Principle" (9).

5. Bella Kussy in "The Vitalist Trend and Thomas Wolfe," *Sewanee Review* 50 (1942): 306–24, notes that "there is an inherent tendency [in vitalism] to run over into an unrestrained dynamism, in which 'life' becomes a force of vio-lent and terrific intensity" (102). In connecting this philosophy to Wolfe, Kussy notes, "The world of Thomas Wolfe is a vital, animate world" (102), and "Wolfe's characters . . . are preeminently alive, not in the realistic sense of being 'true to life' so much as in the vitalistic sense of throbbing and overflowing and bursting with dynamic energy" (102). This notion of unrestrained dynamism has been problematic, however, when applied to the political sphere. Specifi-cally, Kussy and others, such as Richard Kennedy, note that the vitalistic view has sometimes been misappropriated to legitimize the notion that the strong are "better" than the weak, thus loaning false intellectual support to move-ments such as fascism and Nazism. They are at pains to point out, however, that Wolfe eventually saw such brutish political ideology as a misguided appli-cation of vitalism, basing his conclusions on his observations of the Nazi state in Germany and the oppression of the weak in the modern urban society.

6. This dual treatment of the environment is equally evident in Wolfe's nonfiction. In an essay addressing Wolfe's *A Western Journal: A Daily Log of the Great Parks Trip June 20–July 2 1938* (Pittsburgh, Pa.: University of Pittsburgh Press, 1967, Shawn Holliday refers to Wolfe's use of two different discourses, "scientific" and "artistic," which are analogous to objective and subjective, respectively: "Several times in his journal, Wolfe jumps back and forth between both types of language, creating ruptures in the text that verify his attempt to categorize his surroundings into a meaningful whole" (39). Thus, during Wolfe's trip through the western national parks in the summer of 1938, he not only studied and recorded the actual geography of the landscape, but also tried to conjure its essence with his art. For example, in the section of his journal where he recalls "the desert, sage brush, and bare, naked hills, giant-molded, crater-ous, cupreous, glaciated blasted—a demonic heath with reaches of great pine"

(5), the "giant-molded" and "demonic" attributes serve as Wolfe's imaginative claim on a scene he has otherwise described in naturalistic terms. In fact, just as the great impressionist artists also had the ability to draw and paint objects in concrete, representational terms, so Wolfe the environmental impressionist also had the ability to describe environmental phenomena in "scientific," objective terms: "A great butterfly, with wings of blue velvet streaked with gold and scarlet markings, fluttered heavily before them in freckled sunlight, tottering to rest finally upon a spray of dogwood" (LHA, 376). Hugh Holman goes so far as to suggest that southern writers demonstrate an acculturated valuation of concreteness: "This use of the particular, this tendency to distrust the conceptual and abstract, is one of the most widely recognized characteristics of southern writing" (Loneliness, 114).

7. Perhaps Dos Passos' surreal images of the city in Manhattan Transfer (Boston: Houghton Mifflin, 1925) come closest to matching Wolfe's transfigured images of the city.

8. In a letter to Elizabeth Lemmon (November 8, 1934) in The Letters of Thomas Wolfe, ed. Elizabeth Nowell (New York: Charles Scribner's Sons, 1956), Wolfe announced, "I've got to find my America somewhere here in Brooklyn and Manhattan, in all the fog and swelter of the city, in subways and railway stations, on trains and in the Chicago Stock Yards" (LTW, 425). In Of Time and the River, Eugene Gant comes to the same conclusion after having spent a weekend in the pastoral setting of the Pierce estate on the Hudson:

> It was a desperate and soul-sickening discovery to know that not alone through moonlight, magic, and the radiant images of their heart's desire could men find America, but that somewhere there, and far darklier and strangelier than the river, lay the thing they sought . . . buried in the grimy and illimitable jungles of its savage cities. (571)

9. For a discussion of Wolfe's oppositional style, see Holman, Loneliness, 116.

10. Wolfe's personification of the city was his own contribution to what was then a revolutionary approach in early twentieth-century American fiction: "As the twentieth century opens . . . a reinterpretation of the city begins to emerge in the novels of certain American writers who are particularly sensitive social observers of the influence of urbanization upon the individual psyche" (Jane Augustine, "From Topos to Anthropoid: The City as Character in Twentieth-Century Texts," in City Images: Perspectives from Literature, Philosophy, and Film,

ed. Mary Ann Caws (New York: Gordon and Breach, 1991): 73. One of the results of this literary movement was that "the city [became] less a *topos* and more anthropoid—'man-like,' 'resembling the human being,' more organic and seemingly capable of choice. It [became] quasi-human" (74).

11. Wolfe's hopeful visions of America were also shared by Hart Crane and Carl Sandburg. While Crane failed to sustain the credibility of his affirmative images in "The Bridge," in *The Collected Poems of Hart Crane,* ed. Waldo Frank (New York: Liveright, 1933): 3–58, a poem which was intended to counteract Eliot's fatalism in "The Waste Land" in *The Waste Land and Other Poems* (New York: Harcourt Brace Jovanovich, 1962), Sandburg successfully communicated his faith in America by illuminating positive scenes from both rural and urban spaces, a method similar to Wolfe's. For example, in Sandburg's "Chicago" in *The Complete Poems of Carl Sandburg* (New York: Harcourt Brace Jovanovich, 1970): 3–4, he leavens his dark personification of the city—"They tell me you are wicked and I believe them, for I have seen your / painted women under gas lamps luring farm boys" (6–7)—with a transcendent persona which is vital, powerful, and proud: "Come and show me another city with lifted head singing so proud to be / alive and coarse and strong and cunning" (14–15). Although both Wolfe and Sandburg would have agreed with Nick Carraway's assessment that America had, indeed, fallen from its mythical greatness—that its institutions had betrayed the best that is in Americans—they nurtured the faith that the seeds of redemption resided in the still-vital integrity of the American earth and its ordinary citizens. See also Robert Raynolds, *Thomas Wolfe: Memoir of a Friendship* (Austin: University of Texas Press, 1964), for Wolfe's comments about America's distinctive "light" (100).

12. The impression that protagonists and speakers share a common consciousness in Wolfe's texts is based on their similar diction, references, imagery, and catch phrases. In fact, according to Hugh Holman, "we are apparently justified in saying that, after 1930, Wolfe instinctively wrote in the first person, and that the appearance of the bulk of his work after *Look Homeward, Angel* in the third person represents editorial not authorial decision" (*Loneliness,* 78). This suggests that Wolfe's tendency was to address narratological issues via the subjective impressions of his primary protagonists. In fact, all of *Of Time and the River* was converted by editor John Hall Wheelock to the third person from its original first person point of view, and the manuscript that contained *The Web and the Rock* and *You Can't Go Home Again* was interspersed with various sections in the first person which were converted by editor Edward Aswell to

a consistent third person point of view. However, despite these conversions to third person, Wolfe's narrators still speak either from the protagonists' perspectives—"The Spring drove a thorn into his heart, it drew a wild cry from his lips. For it, he had no speech" (*LHA,* 250)—or as their proxies. In the latter case, the narrative voice, as an extension of the protagonist's consciousness, expresses what the protagonist's sentiments would be like if he were immediately present. For example, the lengthy and celebrated paean to the Hudson River in chapter 58 of *Of Time and the River* ("And in the night time, in the dark there, in all the sleeping silence of the earth have we not heard the river, the rich immortal river, full of its strange dark time?" [510]) is a thematic complement to Eugene's poetic observations and musings about the river in chapter 60 ("and then he would see the dark and sleeping woods of night . . . and the velvet-breasted mystery of the strange and silent river . . . drawing on forever like time and silence past the strange and secret land, the mysterious earth" [526]). The presence of a shared consciousness between these passages is supported by their homogenous elements; both invoke landscapes whose literal and figurative elements consist of the river, the nighttime, the earth, time, and mystery. Thus, the consciousness of a Wolfe protagonist is omnipresent throughout its text, capable of manifesting as different modes of expression at different moments and in different contexts.

13. An example of the vitality of the psyche overwhelming the vitality of the environment is when George Webber first comes to the city and "sees" it through the imaginative mental template that he has built up over the years: "the great city is within him, encysted in his heart, built up in all the flaming images of his brain" (*WR,* 212).

14. In emotionalizing the landscape, Wolfe also uses the environment in his texts as a bellwether of the emotional tone of a narrative segment, much as a musical prologue foreshadows the theme of a composition. For instance, the rebirth of spring which opens chapter 38 in *Look Homeward, Angel*—"The leaves were out in a tender green blur: the quilled jonquil spouted from the rich black earth, and peach-blossom fell upon the shrill young isles of grass. Everywhere life was returning, awaking, reviving" (487)—is confluent with the subsequent vignettes of Eugene's own reawakening to life after his wintertime of mourning. Similarly, the celebrated "October had come again" passage, which opens chapter 39 of *Of Time and the River,* sets the tone of both loss and renewal that resonates through the remaining chapters of Book III ("Telemachus").

15. While in this case the land impresses its character on a native son, in Wolfe's play, *The Mountains,* ed. Pat M. Ryan (Chapel Hill: University of North

Carolina Press, 1970), human character is impressed on the land: "In the middle distance, apparently isolated from other mountains, is a granite peak, a curious natural malformation, whose stark outlines suggest strangely the profile of an old, hook-nosed, sardonically grinning man" (94). This mountain peak is further "humanized" by being called "Bald Pate."

16. Williams, a contemporary of Wolfe, attests to the ecological relationship between landscape-making and consciousness-making when he figures the shaping of a city and its inhabitants as a form of organic co-gestation: "rolling up out of chaos,/a nine months' wonder, the city/the man, an identity—it can't be/otherwise—an/interpenetration, both ways" ("Preface," *Paterson,* ed. Christopher MacGowan [New York: New Directions, 1992]: 21–25).

Chapter 3

1. In 1906 Wolfe went with his mother to live at her newly purchased Asheville boarding house, the Old Kentucky Home, at 48 Spruce Street. His father continued to live at Woodfin Street. Despite the separation between the parents, Wolfe continued to spend a lot of time at his father's house. The embowered nature of the house at Woodfin Street was suggested by the mass of grape vines which wound up the front porch. Mabel Wheaton, one of Wolfe's sisters in *Thomas Wolfe and His Family* (New York: Doubleday, 1961), recalls:

> The front porch sat high above the ground and below it a lacelike wooden lattice shielded the brick underpinnings. Over this lattice and up to the eaves of the porch ran grapevines. When the grapes were ripe we could stand on the porch and pick them. Many a time I climbed onto the banisters and, holding to a porch column with one hand, with the other picked great clusters hanging from the porch-roof gutters. (17)

2. See Thomas Wolfe, *The Mountains,* which consists of the one- and three-act versions of Wolfe's play by the same title. Both versions, which were performed in 1921, begin with mountain vistas. Scene-setting for the one-act version includes the description, "Through the window of the back may be seen a stretch of green valley land and reaching across in the distance a panorama of great wooded mountains" (54); and, following a "Prologue" that states, "Receding into the mists at the horizon's edge are interlapping ranges of blue mountains" (87), scene-setting for Act I of the three-act version includes the description, "through the broad windows of the back a view of the mountain

landscape is disclosed burnished by the red glow of the sun which is just dropping behind the horizon" (94).

3. In "The Rock in Maine" scene in *The Hound of Darkness,* ed. John L. Idol Jr. (Rocky Mount, N.C.: Walker-Ross, 1986), Wolfe uses the sea and namesake rock to dramatize how nature's enduring presence makes it the quintessential touchstone in a world where human history and human life do not hold still. We are told, "Upon the rock, two voices and two figures, a woman's and a man's" (131), after which the woman's voice says, "It seems so long a time since we were here. . . . Thinking about this rock in years that passed I thought of you." At the end of the scene, in words that serve to both consecrate and symbolize their mutual desire to maintain an enduring love, the woman's voice says, "And the sea shall not alter" (134), and the man's voice immediately responds in refrain, "The rock shall not break."

4. While mountains were arguably Wolfe's favorite icon of perdurability, he treated rivers as embodying both the fixity *and* flow of time. Thus, Wolfe's mantric description of the Hudson "as it flows by us, by us, to the sea" (*OTR,* 510) is used to suggest both time passing and time arrested in infinite, flowing repetition.

5. Wolfe's apprehension of an indifferent natural world—in the tradition of American naturalism—is implicit in his observations of a ship and its passengers during a storm at sea, observations that recall Stephen Crane's famous representation of the sea—and by extension, the universe—in his story, "The Open Boat," in *The Complete Short Stories and Sketches of Stephen Crane,* ed. Thomas A. Gullason (Garden City, N.Y.: Doubleday & Company, 1963):

> They feel the great hull in the dark plunge down into the heaving waste, and instantly they feel the terrible presence of miles of water below them, and the limitless, howling, mutable desert of the sea around them.
>
> The great ship, as if pressed down by some gigantic finger from the sky, plunged up and down in that living immortal substance which gave before it, but which gave like an infinite feel of mercury, with no suggestion of defeat, giving to itself and returning to itself unmarred, without loss of change, with the terrible indifference of eternity. (*WR,* 282)

6. In a letter to his brother Fred (June 2, 1930), Wolfe expressed this same notion—that a place of human habitation is ultimately defined by, and derives its greatest value from, its natural surroundings—in a reference to his hometown:

For many people in the town I feel the greatest affection and respect, but if I ever grow the least bit homesick it is not for the town of Asheville, but for the great and marvellous hills of North Carolina in which I was fortunate enough to be born, and in which Asheville had the good sense to get built. (*LTW,* 230)

7. While Wolfe depicts Eugene as coming to feel a kinship with the sea in *Look Homeward, Angel,* it is a kinship with the sea's alien nature:

O sea! (he thought) I am the hill-born, the prison-pent, the ghost, the stranger, and I walk here at your side. O sea, I am lonely like you, I am strange and far like you, I am sorrowful like you; my brain, my heart, my life, like yours, have touched strange shores. (436)

8. Louis D. Rubin Jr. argues that George Webber's "squeal" primarily reflects his joy at being released temporarily from the constraints of space and time (*Weather,* 71). However, while the squeal does not respond exclusively to the natural world, the natural world has the greatest capacity to elicit George's animal-cries and vitalize his being.

9. See Douglas Johnson, "Eliza Gant's Web: Her Role as Earth Mother and Moral Hub in *The Web of Earth,*" *Thomas Wolfe Review* 18, no. 1 (1994): 42–47, and Cynthia McVey, "Myth in Thomas Wolfe's *The Web of Earth,*" *Thomas Wolfe Review* 8, no. 1 (1984): 53–57, for detailed treatment of the Earth Mother aspects of Eliza Gant's character as revealed in *The Web of Earth.* It should be pointed out, however, that while the Eliza of this story shares the same name as Eugene Gant's mother in *Look Homeward, Angel,* the former Eliza is spiritually bound to the earth while the latter is not and, in fact, the Eliza character of "The Web of Earth" was originally conceived as a distinctively different character named "Delia Hawke." Wolfe's tendency to portray women in the classic role of Earth Mother is evident throughout his work. In a letter to Perkins (July 17, 1930) in which he explains his proposed use of myths in what will become *Of Time and the River,* he notes, "I am making an extensive use of old myths in my book . . . You know already that I am using the Heracles . . . and Antaeus myth; and you know that the lords of fructification and the earth are almost always women: Maya in the Eastern Legends; Demeter in the Greek; Ceres in Latin, etc." (*LTW,* 243–44). Accordingly, Wolfe characterizes Rosalind Pierce as being "lovely, sweet and strong as the whole earth around her" (*OTR,* 525), and mythologizes Mrs. Selborne as "the dim vast figure of love and maternity,

ageless and autumnal, waiting, corn-haired . . . in the ripe fields of harvest—
Demeter, Helen, the ripe exhaustless and renewing energy" (*LHA*, 121).

10. This story is based on a visit that Wolfe's mother made to his home in
Brooklyn in 1932. In a gesture whose probable motivation—to reconnect her
son to his native earth—is remarkably similar to Eliza's at the end of this story,
Julia Wolfe once sent her Brooklynite son a shipment of homegrown grapes.
Although most were bruised during transport, Wolfe reports in a letter (Sep-
tember 26, 1933) that they still smelled of home: "The grapes, I am sorry to say,
were reduced almost to a mass of rotting pulp, there were a few good ones and
I picked out as many as I could, enough to get the taste and flavor of home
again" (*LTM*, 213).

11. Perhaps Wolfe's harshest appraisal of a life lived apart from nature is
reserved for failed and embittered artists, whom he views as being, by defini-
tion, anti-life (anti-nature) in spirit. As such, they live "rootless, earthless, sun-
less lives" (*OTR*, 289).

12. See Thomas E. Boyle, "Thomas Wolfe: Theme through Imagery," *Modern
Fiction Studies* 11 (1965): 259–68, and "Frederick Jackson Turner and Thomas
Wolfe: The Frontier as History and as Literature" (1970).

13. In a postcard to his mother (July 18, 1929) sent from Ocean Point,
Maine, Wolfe wrote that he was staying at "a little place on the wild and rocky
Maine coast with few summer cottages. I hear the sea all day and all night—I
sleep on the porch of a cottage right in the spruce woods, not 25 yards away
from the water. . . . A great place to get a rest" (*LTM*, 149). In a subsequent letter to his mother (July 28, 1929), he announced, "If I ever make any money I
may buy or build a little place here" (149). However, while Wolfe acted on his
own "back to nature" impulses, he derided those return-to-the-country enthu-
siasts whom he felt were escaping from life rather than being earnestly drawn
to nature. The "back to nature" movement, which crested between the 1880s
and the 1920s, appealed to urbanites' desire for spiritual nourishment (Schmitt,
xvii–xviii). With this movement in mind, Wolfe chose, in *You Can't Go Home
Again*, to portray the Reades, the people whose home is "The House in the
Country" where George Webber and Lloyd McHarg stay overnight, as escapists
rather than nature-lovers: "For Rickenbach Reade, George began to see after a
while, was one of those men who are unequal to the conditions of modern life,
and who have accordingly retreated from the tough realities which they could
not face" (*YCGHA*, 467).

14. The phrase, "machine in the garden," refers to Leo Marx's *The Machine in the Garden* (New York: Oxford University Press, 1977). He uses the words "machine" and "garden" to stand for urbanization and the natural world, respectively.

15. The celebrated phrase, "a stone, a leaf, a door," which was adapted by Wolfe from a passage from Book III of Wordsworth's "The Prelude" (1850), refers to the scope of Wordsworth's eyesight:

> for I had an eye
> Which in my strongest workings, evermore
> Was looking for the shades of difference
> As they hid in all exterior forms,
> Near or remote, minute or vast, an eye
> Which, from a tree, a stone, a withered leaf,
> To the broad ocean and the azure heavens
> Spangled with kindred multitudes of stars
> Could find no surface where its power might sleep.
> (lines 156–64)

While the "door" refers either to the gateway to a preexistent world or a welcome entry into life, scholars have viewed the "leaf" as referring to human mortality and the "stone" as representing, among other things, "the immobility of the earth" (Margaret Church, "Thomas Wolfe: Dark Time," in *Thomas Wolfe: Three Decades of Criticism*, ed. Leslie A. Field [New York: New York University Press, 1968]: 85–103) and "the angel which dominates not only the title but the text of the first novel" (E. K. Brown, "Thomas Wolfe: Realist and Symbolist," 219). In viewing Wolfe's treatment of these objects of nature from an ecocritical perspective, the stone and the leaf may also be seen to symbolize the enduring and cyclical aspects, respectively, of the natural world.

16. See Thomas Wolfe, "The Return of Buck Gavin: The Tragedy of a Mountain Outlaw" (1924).

17. In an interview with the *Asheville Times* (May 4, 1930), Wolfe, then living in New York City, is quoted as saying, "I am proud of my family, and I still consider Asheville my home. New York is certainly not. I like it, but it is a giant of steel and stone far different from the open spaces where a man can plant his feet on caressing earth and breathe" (Aldo Magi and Richard Walser, eds. *Thomas Wolfe Interviewed: 1929–1938* [Baton Rouge: Louisiana State University Press, 1985]).

Chapter 4

1. In fact, if it were possible to quantify the number, type, and frequency of nature references in Wolfe's tetralogy, it would be clear that the "nature index" decreases, albeit unevenly, as one progresses from *Look Homeward, Angel* through *You Can't Go Home Again.*

2. Wolfe's use of nature to textually frame human narratives is especially dramatized by several self-contained scenes in *The Hound of Darkness*. For example, in "The Mexicans" (41–46) and "The Lovers" (35–38), images of the moon and other tokens of nature both precede and succeed the human action.

3. See also "The Lovers" scene in Wolfe's *The Hound of Darkness,* which dramatizes this "leaf chorus" scenario more extensively.

4. It cannot be overemphasized how much Wolfean moonlight serves as a critical environmental device, as Wolfe used it virtually everywhere to signify the ubiquitous presence of nature in human affairs. This figurative treatment is especially overt in *The Hound of Darkness,* where all scenes are cast in the moon's light, as advertised by the prologue: "Scene: A night of dazzling light above America" (4), "The Night of June 18, 1916:—A Full Moon."

5. Louis D. Rubin Jr. points out that Wolfe also viewed the coming of spring as a unsettling reminder of his own mortality. Rubin notes, "The coming of spring thus becomes more terrible by the very beauty of the tree and nature" (*Weather,* 35), and "it is the advent of spring, with its connotations of the perennial and everlasting rebirth of the seasons, that seems to touch off all [Wolfe's] fears and regrets, and his sense of futility in the face of the solstice's ruthless coming, in despite of the petty woes of mortality" (36).

6. Wolfe's figuring of the city, variously, as human-made and nature-made, can be problematic in terms of its changing identity, recalling Blanche Gelfant's comment that Wolfe "could not bring order to his use of this [city] symbol" (131). For instance, when New York City's human-made identity is foregrounded, its transience is juxtaposed to the earth's permanence; however, when its nature-made (rock-like) identity is foregrounded, the city's immutable earth is juxtaposed to the mutable Hudson river, time arrested juxtaposed to time passing. The city is also figured at times as a mutable river itself, embodied by the flow of human traffic in its midst.

7. Wolfe himself, especially his height, inspired nature similes in those who tried to characterize his imposing physical stature. When Shelby Foote

first saw Wolfe in 1937 on the University of North Carolina campus, he drew on non-sentient nature imagery to describe him "as a giant California sequoia" (Samway, *Walker Percy: A Life*).

8. While this passage serves as an appropriate conclusion to Wolfe's treatment of nature throughout his tetralogy, these lines were, in fact, transposed from Wolfe's essay, "I Have a Thing to Tell You" (1937), by Edward Aswell in "A Note on Thomas Wolfe," afterward to *The Hills Beyond*, by Thomas Wolfe. (Reprint, New York: New American Library, 1968): 271–304.

Chapter 5

1. See Jimmie Carol Still Durr, *"Look Homeward, Angel*, Thomas Wolfe's *Ulysses," Southern Studies* 24, no. 1 (1985): 54–68.

2. Louis D. Rubin Jr.'s emphasis on the sensual freshness of *Look Homeward, Angel* borrows from Wordsworth's notion (best expressed in his "Intimations of Immortality" [1807]) that since we saw things more vividly as children, our remembrances from that period will be more vivid as well. After *Look Homeward, Angel*, notes Rubin, "we get three novels which in varying degrees lack perspective, lack dimension, and lack the rich representation of life in space, color, and time that *Look Homeward, Angel* afforded" (*Weather*, 152–53).

3. Wolfe's treatment of modernist issues and themes is more salient in *Look Homeward, Angel* at the individual and familial level than at the societal level, the latter being more pronounced in his later novels, which take place primarily in the modernist city. Thus, Wolfe addresses social fragmentation by dramatizing the Gants' "house divided" and the disconnections between family members; addresses alienation by highlighting Ben's and Eugene's outsider status, aloneness, and loneliness; and addresses the gulf between men and women by dramatizing the chasm between Gant and Eliza, Helen and Hugh Barton.

4. Thoreau wrote, "The West of which I speak is but another name for the Wild ("The Wild," in *Thoreau's Vision*, ed. Charles R. Anderson [Englewood Cliffs, N.J.: Prentice-Hall, 1973]: 144). The West is also the Thoreauvian direction of freedom and adventure:

> It is hard for me to believe that I shall find fair landscapes or sufficient wildness and freedom behind the eastern horizon. . . . I believe that the forest

which I see in the western horizon stretches uninterruptedly toward the setting sun. (139)

We go westward as into the future, with a spirit of enterprise and adventure. (140)

Using the same rhetoric of the West, Gant the Far-Wanderer recalls his "last great voyage" (57) to California: "It was more spacious there. . . . There was width to the eye, a smoking sun-hazed amplitude, the world convoluting and opening into the world, hill and plain, into the west. The West for desire, the East for home" (60).

5. In the initial "Orestes" section of *Of Time and the River,* Eugene's journey from Altamont to Baltimore retraces, in reverse, Gant's initial passage from the lowlands to the mountains, dramatizing the geographical gap which lies between them. The narrator notes that "the physical changes and transitions of the journey are strange and wonderful enough" (25). Another such landscape-altering train ride is the one George Webber takes from New York City to Libya Hill in chapter five of *You Can't Go Home Again.*

6. While Eugene initially sees the mountains as portals to an enchanted world ("Against the hidden other flanks of the immutable hills the world washed like a vast and shadowy sea, alive with the great fish of his imagining" [160]), he also comes to view the circle of mountains as barriers, acknowledging, with a sense of loss, that his "vision of the earth was mountain-walled" (520). In this context, it is interesting to note that, according to John L. Idol Jr., the reception at Harvard of Wolfe's play, *The Mountains,* "disheartened [Wolfe] and left him open to mockery because he had made such an issue of mountains as physical barriers to the outside world" (*Companion,* 92). This dual identity of the mountains—as both portals and barriers—is a theme played throughout Wolfe's oeuvre and exemplified, in *The Hills Beyond,* by the evolution of the Joyner family into country and town branches, located in the "world-lost fastnesses" (182) of Zebulon County and in "the most urban settlement of Libya Hill," respectively:

> Hill-bound, world-lost, locked in the narrow valleys and the mountain walls
> of Zebulon, the Joyners who remained at home became almost as strange and
> far away as if their home had been the Mountains of the Moon. . . . The Libya
> Hill Joyners were facing ever toward the world, and those in Zebulon away
> from it. (183)

Certain imaginative people, however, can see beyond the mountains. Eugene is such a person, and so is one of these same Joyners, Gustavus Adolphus

Joyner: "He looked and saw the hills, and in his kindling vision leaped beyond them. His eyes pierced the mountain wall and swept beyond to daydreams of the golden cities of the plains" (*HB*, 218).

7. *Look Homeward, Angel* features many scenes where daybreak and evening are figured as spiritual salves. Thus, Coleridgeian moonlight is figured as having an antiseptic effect on the land ("The moonlight fell upon the earth like a magic unearthly dawn. It wiped away all rawness, it hid all sores" [368]), and both nascent daylight and darkness are figured as having cleansing effects on the town of Altamont and its inhabitants: "The town emerged from the lilac darkness with a washed renascent cleanliness. All the world seemed as young as Spring" (149); "Darkness melted over the town like dew; it washed out all the day's distress, harsh confusions" (383). The latter "washing" references also exemplify Wolfe's use of water and water imagery to denote purification, as further illustrated when Eugene seeks to anneal his body with mineral water while on a trip through the Ozarks: "He drank endlessly the water that came smoking from the earth, hoping somehow to wash himself clean from all pollution, beginning his everlasting fantasy of the miraculous spring" (132). Also, when Eugene sees Helen's purity in beatific visions, he sees her as "a sky washed by rain" (374).

Chapter 6

1. One of the exceptions to this general oversight of Wolfe's romantic treatment of nature is John Hagan's essay, "The Whole Passionate Enigma of Life: Thomas Wolfe on Nature and the Youthful Quest" (1983).

2. In "The Romantic Tradition: Coleridge and Wolfe, Part I," *Thomas Wolfe Review* 16, no. 1 (1992), David K. Perelman-Hall uses Reid Huntley's "six features of the Romantic character" (21)—all of which fit Wolfe to some degree—to address Wolfe's standing as a romantic:

> 1) A stress on the creative imagination that modifies and changes materials from the active world before it becomes art; 2) A stress on innate genius; 3) The expression (or self-expression) of an author's passions and subjective responses to his materials; 4) The centrality of the notions of organic unity and organic growth, in contrast to mechanical unity; 5) A belief in the reality of things in the ideal world such as supernatural appearances, and 6) use of symbolic language and objects to convey abstract meanings and to heighten their significance beyond the literal or actual meaning. (21)

3. Karl Kroeber addresses the inadequacy of contemporary criticism to address the ecological implications of romantic literature. Specifically, he exposes the homocentric bias against reading the romantics' references to nature in their poems as overt commentaries on humankind's place in the natural world (*Ecological Literary Criticism: Romantic Imagining and the Biology of Mind* [New York: Columbia University Press, 1994]: 2). Jonathan Bate draws attention to this bias when he points out that in the 1960s there was a critical movement to privilege the imagination of romanticism over its focus on nature. This movement was, in turn, supplanted in the 1980s by those who wanted to conceive romanticism in primarily ideological terms (*Romantic Ecology: Wordsworth and the Environmental Tradition* [New York: Routledge, 1991]: 9).

4. According to Kroeber, the romantic poets were "forerunners of a new biological, materialistic understanding of humanity's place in the natural cosmos" (*Ecological*, 2).

5. Seeing the miraculous in the common was, of course, one of the tenets of Wordsworth's aesthetic philosophy as enunciated in his poetic manifesto, the "Preface to *Lyrical Ballads*" (1802).

6. According to M. H. Abrams, "Life is the premise and paradigm for what is most innovative and distinctive in Romantic thinkers. Hence their vitalism; the celebration of that which lives, moves, and evolves by an internal energy, over what ever is lifeless, inert, and unchanging" (*Natural Supernaturalism* [New York: Norton, 1971]: 431).

7. In a letter to Maxwell Perkins (July 1, 1930) in which he addressed this flood scene, Wolfe writes the following observation about Furman's wife: "The whole scene, told in the woman's homely speech, moves to the rhythm of the great river. . . . You understand that the river is in her brain, in her thought, in her speech. . . . And she hates the river, but all its sounds are in her brain, she cannot escape it" (*LTW,* 239).

8. The romantics believed that the primary purpose of a poem was to induce pleasurable feelings: "What the successes of late twentieth-century critics have disastrously obscured is the British romantic poets' extraordinary emphasis on *pleasure* as the foundation of poetry, even political verse" (Kroeber, *Ecological,* 5).

9. Perelman-Hall notes, "Wolfe granted to life, to the earth even, a profound organic unity based on notions he drew from Coleridge, or at least from the nineteenth-century Romantic poets" (79).

10. Interestingly, the personal and emotional coloration of Wordsworth's responses to nature attracted the same kind of criticism and misunderstanding that were leveled at Wolfe's subjectivism: "Wordsworth opened himself to the charge of 'egoism' because characteristically he did not present himself in his poetry as an 'objective' observer" (Kroeber, *Ecological,* 80).

11. Wolfe's ambivalent vision of nature, which Holman describes as "a Manichaean cosmic view" (*Loneliness,* 33), was also shared by Wordsworth (Kroeber, *Ecological,* 47).

12. See Hagan's overview of Wolfe's secular faith in nature (32).

13. Coleridge asserted that art "is the mediatress between, and reconciler of, nature and man," and that "to make the external internal, the internal external, to make nature thought, and thought nature—this is the mystery of genius in the Fine Arts" (Abrams, 269).

14. This same "organic" method was practiced by the romantics in their poetry and best popularized by Coleridge. J. R. Watson notes, "Organic form . . . develops freely from the subject and the poet's treatment of it, and contains no received or preconceived elements" (*English Poetry of the Romantic Period: 1789–1830,* 2d. ed. [New York: Longman, 1992]: 22). Wolfe's metaphorical use of nature is also consonant with the romantics' practices. Abrams notes the romantics' tendency toward the "metaphorical translation into the categories and norms of intellection of the attributes of a growing thing, which unfolds its inner form and assimilates to itself alien elements, until it reaches the fullness of its complex, organic unity" (432).

15. My claims concerning the similar writing ideologies of Cather and Hemingway are based on Glen Love's essay, "*The Professor's House:* Cather, Hemingway, and the Chastening of American Prose Style," *Western American Literature* 24 (1990): 295–311.

16. By contrast, in "Neighbor Rosicky" (1932), the landscape and the emotional tone of the narrative are both domesticated by bland phrases such as, "Well, it was a nice snowstorm" (*Five Stories,* [New York: Vintage Books, 1956]: 81), and "The fine snow . . . looked very pretty" (81).

17. The one-with-nature experiences of Godfrey St. Peter (*The Professor's House* [New York: Knopf, 1925] and Jean Marie Latour (Willa Cather, *Death Comes for the Archbishop* [New York: Knopf, 1926]) are similarly conveyed, according to Carol Steinhagen, via a confusion of intellectual rather than emotional boundaries.

18. In his essay, "Environment as Meaning: John Steinbeck and the Great Central Valley," *Steinbeck Quarterly* 10, no. 1 (1977), Jackson J. Benson notes, "It is remarkable just how little of the Great Valley, from this point on in the novel [when the Joads first enter the valley], is ever described in any detail, emphasizing the lack of substantial contact by the Joads with the valley itself" (15).

19. While the disjunctions in *The Grapes of Wrath* between the narrator's and characters' perceptions and between the characters and their surroundings are useful, comparatively, for distinguishing Wolfe's subjective window on the natural world and his representation of greater emotional contact with it, it is also true that Steinbeck has written other texts where a more subjective point of view yields a greater sense of closeness with the nonhuman world. See, for example, Jody's impressions of the natural world in Steinbeck's *The Red Pony* (New York: Viking Press, 1945).

20. The reincarnation of the "buried men" into "flower and leaf" especially contradicts the Stetson section of "The Waste Land": "'That corpse you planted last year in your garden, / 'Has it begun to sprout? Will it bloom this year?" (71–72).

21. While "Mid-Day" and "Loss" were originally published in 1916 and "Oread" in 1915, their texts were again in circulation among the poetic community in the 1920s in the *Collected Poems of H. D.* (Reprint, New York: Liveright, 1940).

Bibliography

Works by Thomas Wolfe

Antaeus, or A Memory of Earth. Edited by Ted Mitchell. Rocky Mount, N.C.: Walker-Ross, 1996.

The Complete Short Stories of Thomas Wolfe. Edited by Francis E. Skipp. New York: Scribner, 1987.

The Face of a Nation. New York: Charles Scribner's Sons, 1939.

From Death to Morning. 1935. Reprint, New York: Charles Scribner's Sons, 1970.

The Hills Beyond. 1941. Reprint, New York: New American, 1968.

The Hound of Darkness. Edited by John L. Idol Jr. Rocky Mount, N.C.: Walker-Ross, 1986.

"I Have a Thing to Tell You." *New Republic,* 10 March 1937, 132–36; 17 March 1937, 159–64; 24 March 1937, 202–7.

The Letters of Thomas Wolfe. Edited by Elizabeth Nowell. New York: Charles Scribner's Sons, 1956.

The Letters of Thomas Wolfe to His Mother. Edited by Hugh C. Holman and Sue Fields Ross. Chapel Hill: University of North Carolina Press, 1968.

Look Homeward, Angel. 1929. Reprint, New York: Charles Scribner's Sons, 1957.

The Mountains. Edited by Pat M. Ryan. Chapel Hill: University of North Carolina Press, 1970.

My Other Loneliness: Letters of Thomas Wolfe and Aline Bernstein. Edited by Suzanne Stutman. Chapel Hill: University of North Carolina Press, 1983.

The Notebooks of Thomas Wolfe. Vol. 2. Edited by Richard S. Kennedy and Paschal Reeves. Chapel Hill: University of North Carolina Press, 1970.

Of Time and the River. New York: Charles Scribner's Sons, 1935.

Return. Asheville, N.C.: Thomas Wolfe Memorial, 1976.

"The Return of Buck Gavin: The Tragedy of a Mountain Outlaw." *Carolina Folk-Plays.* Ed. Frederick H. Koch. New York: Holt, Rinehart & Winston, 1924.

A Stone, a Leaf, a Door. Comp. John S. Barnes. New York: Charles Scribner's Sons, 1969.

The Story of a Novel. New York: Charles Scribner's Sons, 1936.

The Web and the Rock. 1939. Reprint, New York: Perennial Library, 1973.

A Western Journal: A Daily Log of the Great Parks Trip June 20–July 2, 1938 (1951). Pittsburgh, Pa.: University of Pittsburgh Press, 1967.

You Can't Go Home Again. 1940. Reprint, New York: Perennial Library, 1989.

Works by Others

Abrams, M. H. *Natural Supernaturalism.* New York: Norton, 1971.

Adams, Agatha Boyd. *Thomas Wolfe, Carolina Student: A Brief Biography.* Chapel Hill: University of North Carolina Library, 1955.

Armstrong, Anne W. "As I Saw Thomas Wolfe." *Arizona Quarterly* 2 (1946): 5–15.

Aswell, Edward C. "A Note on Thomas Wolfe." Afterword to *The Hills Beyond,* by Thomas Wolfe. 1941. Reprint, New York: New American Library, 1968.

Augustine, Jane. "From Topos to Anthropoid: The City as Character in Twentieth-Century Texts." In *City Images: Perspectives from Literature, Philosophy, and Film,* edited by Mary Ann Caws, 73–86. New York: Gordon and Breach, 1991.

Bassett, John E. *Thomas Wolfe: An Annotated Critical Bibliography.* Lanham, Md.: Scarecrow, 1996.

Basso, Hamilton. "Thomas Wolfe." In *After the Genteel Tradition: American Writers Since 1910,* edited by Malcolm Cowley, 202–12. New York: Norton, 1937.

Bate, Jonathan. *Romantic Ecology: Wordsworth and the Environmental Tradition.* New York: Routledge, 1991.

Beach, Joseph Warren. *American Fiction: 1920–1940.* New York: Russell & Russell, 1941.

Beja, Morris. "Thomas Wolfe: The Escapes of Time and Memory." In *Epiphany in the Modern Novel.* Seattle: University of Washington Press, 1971.

Benson, Jackson J. "Environment as Meaning: John Steinbeck and the Great Central Valley." *Steinbeck Quarterly* 10, no. 1 (1977): 12–20.

Bentz, Joseph. "The Influence of Modernist Structure in the Short Fiction of Thomas Wolfe." *Studies in Short Fiction* 31 (1994): 149–61.

Boyer, James D. "The City in the Short Fiction of Thomas Wolfe." *Thomas Wolfe Review* 7, no. 2 (1983): 36–40.

Boyle, Thomas E. "Frederick Jackson Turner and Thomas Wolfe: The Frontier as History and as Literature." *Western American Literature* 4 (1970): 273–85.

———. "Thomas Wolfe: Theme through Imagery." *Modern Fiction Studies* 11 (1965): 259–68.

Bredahl, A. Carl Jr. *New Ground: Western American Narrative and the Literary Canon.* Chapel Hill: University of North Carolina Press, 1989.

Brown, E. K. "Thomas Wolfe: Realist and Symbolist." In *The Enigma of Thomas Wolfe: Biographical and Critical Selections,* edited by Richard Walser, 206–21. Cambridge, Mass.: Harvard University Press, 1953. Originally published in *University of Toronto Quarterly* (January 1941).

Brown, Kenneth. "Thomas Wolfe—A Critical Visit." *Thomas Wolfe Review* 8, no. 1 (1984): 43–52.

Buell, Lawrence. *The Environmental Imagination: Thoreau, Nature Writing, and the Formation of American Culture.* Cambridge, Mass.: Harvard University Press, 1995.

Cather, Willa. *Death Comes for the Archbishop.* New York: Knopf, 1926.

———. *Five Stories.* New York: Vintage Books, 1956.

———. *My Ántonia.* 1918. Reprint, Boston: Houghton Mifflin, 1988.

———. *The Professor's House.* New York: Knopf, 1925.

Church, Margaret. "Thomas Wolfe: Dark Time." In *Thomas Wolfe: Three Decades of Criticism,* edited by Leslie A. Field, 85–103. New York: New York University Press, 1968. Originally published in *Time and Reality: Studies in Contemporary Fiction,* 207–26.

Clarke, Graham. "A 'Sublime and Atrocious' Spectacle: New York and the Iconography of Manhattan Island." In *The American City: Literary and Cultural Perspectives,* edited by Graham Clarke, 36–61. New York: St. Martin's, 1988.

Clayton, Lawrence. "An Example of Ambiguous Imagery in *You Can't Go Home Again.*" *Thomas Wolfe Review* 3, no. 1 (1979): 15–17.

Cobb, Edith. "The Ecology of Imagination in Childhood." In *The Subversive Science,* edited by David McKinley and Paul Shepard, 122–32. Boston: Houghton Mifflin, 1969.

Crane, Hart. "The Bridge." In *The Collected Poems of Hart Crane,* edited by Waldo Frank, 3–58. New York: Liveright, 1933.

Crane, Stephen. "The Open Boat." In *The Complete Short Stories and Sketches of Stephen Crane,* edited by Thomas A. Gullason, 339–59. Garden City, N.Y.: Doubleday & Company, 1963.

Culleton, Claire A. "Joycean Synchronicity in Wolfe's *Look Homeward, Angel.*" *Thomas Wolfe Review* 13, no. 1 (1989): 49–52.

DeVoto, Bernard. "Genius Is Not Enough." *Saturday Review of Literature,* 25 April 1936, 3–4, 14–15.

Dickey, James. Foreword to *The Complete Short Stories of Thomas Wolfe.* Edited by Francis E. Skipp. New York: Scribner, 1987, ix–xv.

Dickstein, Felice Witztum. "The Role of the City in the Works of Theodore Dreiser, Thomas Wolfe, James T. Farrell, and Saul Bellow." Ph.D. diss., City University of New York, 1973.

Donald, David Herbert. *Look Homeward: A Life of Thomas Wolfe.* Boston: Little, Brown & Co., 1987.

———. "Look Homeward: Thomas Wolfe and the South." *Southern Review* 23 (1987): 241–55.

Doolittle, Hilda (H. D.) *Collected Poems of H. D.* 1925. Reprint, New York: Liveright, 1940.

———. *Red Rose for Bronze.* New York: Houghton Mifflin, 1931.

Dos Passos, John. *Manhattan Transfer.* Boston: Houghton Mifflin, 1925.

Douglas, Ann. *Terrible Honesty: Mongrel Manhattan in the 1920s.* New York: Farrar, Straus & Giroux, 1995.

Durr, Jimmie Carol Still. "*Look Homeward, Angel,* Thomas Wolfe's *Ulysses.*" *Southern Studies* 24, no. 1 (1985): 54–68.

Eliot, T. S. *The Waste Land and Other Poems.* New York: Harcourt Brace Jovanovich, 1962.

Emerson, Ralph Waldo. "Nature." In *The Portable Emerson.* Edited by Carl Bode, 7–50. New York: Penguin Books, 1981.

Evernden, Neil. *The Social Creation of Nature.* Baltimore: Johns Hopkins University Press, 1992.

Faulkner, William. *Absalom, Absalom!* 1936. Reprint, New York: Vintage Books, 1964.

———. "The Bear." In *Go Down, Moses.* 1940. Reprint, New York: Vintage Books, 1970.

———. *The Sound and the Fury.* 1929. Reprint, New York: Vintage Books, 1936.

Field, Leslie. "*The Hills Beyond:* A Folk Novel of America." *New York Folklore Quarterly* 16 (1960): 203–15.

———. "*The Web and the Rock:* The City, Esther, and Beyond." *Thomas Wolfe Review* 10, no. 2 (1986): 11–18.

Fitzgerald, F. Scott. *The Great Gatsby.* 1925. Reprint, New York: Macmillan, 1992.

Foster, Ruel E. "Thomas Wolfe: Mountain Gloom and Glory." *American Literature* 44 (1973): 638–47.

Frost, Robert. *The Poetry of Robert Frost.* Edited by Edward Connery Lathem. New York: Holt, Rinehart & Winston, 1969.

Gelfant, Blanche Housman. "The City as Symbol." In *The American City Novel.* Norman: University of Oklahoma Press, 1954.

Glotfelty, Cheryll. Introduction to *The Ecocriticism Reader,* edited by Harold Fromm and Cheryll Glotfelty, xv–xxxvii. Athens: University of Georgia Press, 1996.

Goldsmith, Arnold L. *The Modern American Urban Novel: Nature As 'Interior Structure.'* Detroit, Mich.: Wayne State University Press, 1991.

H., W. E. "A Modern Epic of the Life of a Pennsylvania Youth." Review of *Look Homeward, Angel,* by Thomas Wolfe. *Boston Evening Transcript,* 9 November 1929, 2.

Hagan, John. "'The Whole Passionate Enigma of Life': Thomas Wolfe on Nature and the Youthful Quest." *Thomas Wolfe Review* 7, no. 1 (1983): 32–42.

Hay, John. Preface to *On Nature,* edited by Daniel Halpern. San Francisco: North Point, 1986.

Hemingway, Ernest. *The Green Hills of Africa.* New York: Charles Scribner's Sons, 1935.

———. *In Our Time.* 1925. Reprint, New York: Charles Scribner's Sons, 1958.

———. *The Old Man and the Sea.* New York: Charles Scribner's Sons, 1952.

———. *Ernest Hemingway: Selected Letters, 1917–1961.* Edited by Carlos Baker. New York: Scribner, 1981.

———. *The Sun Also Rises.* 1926. Reprint, New York: Charles Scribner's Sons, 1954.

Hinze, Diana Orendi. "William Faulkner and Thomas Wolfe." *Thomas Wolfe Review* 12, no. 1 (1988): 25–32.

Holliday, Shawn. "The Pity, Terror, Strangeness, and Magnificence of It All: Landscape and Discourse in Thomas Wolfe's *A Western Journal.*" *Thomas Wolfe Review* 21, no. 2 (1997): 34–45.

Holman, Hugh C. *Loneliness at the Core.* Baton Rouge: Louisiana State University Press, 1975.

———. "Thomas Wolfe and America." *Southern Literary Journal* 10, no. 1 (1977): 56–74.

Howell, Elmo. "Thomas Wolfe and the Sense of Place." *South Carolina Review* 11, no. 1 (1978): 96–106.

Idol, John Jr. "Thomas Wolfe and T. S. Eliot: The Hippopotamus and the Old Possum." *Southern Literary Journal* 13, no. 2 (1981): 15–26.

———. *A Thomas Wolfe Companion*. Westport, Conn.: Greenwood, 1987.

Jackson, Joseph Henry. "The Last Work of Thomas Wolfe, Significant Artist of His Time." *San Francisco Chronicle,* 5 July 1939, 13.

Jeffers, Robinson. *The Collected Poetry of Robinson Jeffers.* Vol. 2. Stanford, Calif.: Stanford University Press, 1989.

Johnson, Douglas S. "Eliza Gant's Web: Her Role As Earth Mother and Moral Hub in *The Web of Earth*." *Thomas Wolfe Review* 18, no. 1 (1994): 42–47.

Johnston, Carol Ingalls. *Of Time and the Artist: Thomas Wolfe, His Novels, and the Critics.* Columbia, S.C.: Camden House, 1996.

Joyce, James. *Ulysses.* 1922. Reprint, New York: Vintage Books, 1961.

Kazin, Alfred. *A Writer's America: Landscape in Literature.* New York: Knopf, 1988.

Kennedy, Richard S. *The Window of Memory.* Chapel Hill: University of North Carolina Press, 1962.

Kowalewski, Michael. "Writing in Place: The New American Regionalism." *American Literary History* 6, no. 1 (1994): 171–83.

Kroeber, Karl. *Ecological Literary Criticism: Romantic Imagining and the Biology of Mind.* New York: Columbia University Press, 1994.

———. *Romantic Landscape Vision.* Madison: University of Wisconsin Press, 1975.

Kussy, Bella. "The Vitalist Trend and Thomas Wolfe." *Sewanee Review* 50 (1942): 306–24.

Love, Glen. "*The Professor's House:* Cather, Hemingway, and the Chastening of American Prose Style," *Western American Literature* 24 (1990): 295–311.

———. "Revaluing Nature: Toward an Ecological Criticism." *Western American Literature* 25 (1990): 201–15.

Machor, James L. *Pastoral Cities: Urban Ideals and the Symbolic Landscape of America.* Madison: University of Wisconsin Press, 1987.

Magi, Aldo, and Richard Walser, eds. *Thomas Wolfe Interviewed: 1929–1938.* Baton Rouge: Louisiana State University Press, 1985.

Marx, Leo. *The Machine in the Garden.* New York: Oxford University Press, 1977.

McElderry, B. R. Jr. *Thomas Wolfe.* New York: Twayne, 1964.

McVey, Cynthia. "Myth in Thomas Wolfe's 'The Web of Earth.'" *Thomas Wolfe Review* 8, no. 1 (1984): 53–57.

Meehan, James. "Thomas Wolfe as Regional Historian." *Thomas Wolfe Newsletter* 1, no. 1 (1977): 9–11.

Melville, Herman. *Moby Dick.* 1851. Reprint, New York: Penguin Books, 1992.

Meyer, William E. H. Jr. "Thomas Wolfe's Hypervisual Home." *Thomas Wolfe Review* 11, no. 1 (1987): 4–9.

Moore, Marianne. *Collected Poems.* New York: Macmillan, 1952.

Muller, Herbert J. "Wolfe and the Tradition." In *Thomas Wolfe.* Norfolk, Conn.: New Directions, 1947.

Natanson, Maurice. "The Privileged Moment: A Study in the Rhetoric of Thomas Wolfe." *Quarterly Journal of Speech* 53 (1957): 143–50.

Oakes, Randy W. "Myth and Method: Eliot, Joyce, and Wolfe in *The Web and the Rock.*" *Thomas Wolfe Review* 10, no. 1 (1986): 23–26.

Olson, Charles. *Call Me Ishmael.* New York: Reynal & Hitchcock, 1947.

Perelman-Hall, David K. "The Romantic Tradition: Coleridge and Wolfe, Part 1." *Thomas Wolfe Review* 16, no. 1 (1992): 21–30.

Perkins, Maxwell. "Scribners and Tom Wolfe." In *Always Yours, Max,* edited by Alice R. Cotten, 92–99. Rocky Mount, N.C.: The Thomas Wolfe Society, 1997. Originally published in *Carolina Magazine* 68 (October 1938).

———. Introduction to *Look Homeward, Angel,* by Thomas Wolfe. 1929. Reprint, New York: Charles Scribner's Sons, 1957.

———. "Thomas Wolfe: A Writer for the People of His Time and Tomorrow." *Thomas Wolfe Review* 21, no. 2 (1997): 3–5. Originally published in *Wings* (October 1937).

Quinn, Vincent. *Hilda Doolittle (H. D.).* New York: Twayne, 1967.

Raynolds, Robert. *Thomas Wolfe: Memoir of a Friendship.* Austin: University of Texas Press, 1964.

Reeves, Paschal. "Thomas Wolfe and the Family of Earth." In *The Poetry of Community: Essays on the Southern Sensibility of History and Literature,* edited by Lewis P. Simpson, 47–54. Atlanta: Georgia State University Press, 1972.

Rowe, Anne. "Thomas Wolfe in New York." *Thomas Wolfe Review* 5, no. 1 (1981): 36–41.

Rubin, Louis D. Jr. "Thomas Wolfe and the Place He Came From." *Virginia Quarterly Review* 52 (1976): 183–202.

———. *Thomas Wolfe: The Weather of His Youth.* Baton Rouge: Louisiana State University Press, 1955.

Samway, Patrick H. *Walker Percy: A Life.* New York: Farrar, Straus & Giroux, 1997.

Sandburg, Carl. "Chicago." In *The Complete Poems of Carl Sandburg*. New York: Harcourt Brace Jovanovich, 1970.

Sanders, Scott Russell. "Speaking a Word for Nature." *Michigan Quarterly Review* 26 (1987): 648–62.

Schmitt, Peter J. *Back to Nature: The Arcadian Myth in Urban America*. New York: Oxford University Press, 1969.

Shepard, Paul. *Man in the Landscape: A Historic View of the Esthetics of Nature*. New York: Knopf, 1967.

———. "Place in American Literature." *North American Review* 262, no. 3 (1977): 22–32.

Simpson, Claude. Review of *You Can't Go Home Again,* by Thomas Wolfe. *Southwest Review* 26 (1940): 132–35.

Smrchek, M. N. "*Of Time and the River:* Wolfe, Whitman, and America." *Thomas Wolfe Review* 9, no. 1 (1985): 24–30.

Steinbeck, John. *The Grapes of Wrath* (1939). New York: Viking Press, 1960.

———. *The Red Pony*. New York: Viking Press, 1945.

Steinhagen, Carol. "Dangerous Crossings: Historical Dimensions of Landscape in Willa Cather's *My Ántonia, The Professor's House,* and *Death Comes for the Archbishop.*" *Interdisciplinary Studies in Literature and Environment: ISLE* 6, no. 2 (1999): 63–82.

Stephenson, Shelby. "Elements of Lyricism in *Look Homeward, Angel*." *Thomas Wolfe Review* 20, no. 1 (1996): 79–86.

Stutman, Suzanne. "Home Again: Thomas Wolfe and Pennsylvania." *Resources for American Literary Study* 18, no. 1 (1992): 44–52.

Teicher, Morton I. *Looking Homeward: A Thomas Wolfe Photo Album*. Columbia: University of Missouri Press, 1993.

Thoreau, Henry David. *Walden*. 1854. Reprint, New York: Thomas Y. Crowell, 1966.

———. "The Wild." In *Thoreau's Vision,* edited by Charles R. Anderson, 133–58. Englewood Cliffs, N.J.: Prentice-Hall, 1973.

Wallace, Margaret. "A Novel of Provincial American Life." *New York Times Book Review,* 27 October 1929, 7.

Walser, Richard. "America and Poetry." In *Thomas Wolfe: An Introduction and Interpretation*. New York: Barnes & Noble, 1961.

Watkins, Floyd. "The Sum of All the Moments." In *Thomas Wolfe's Characters: Portraits from Life*. Norman: University of Oklahoma Press, 1957.

Watson, J. R. *English Poetry of the Romantic Period: 1789–1830*. 2d ed. New York: Longman, 1992.

Wheaton, Mabel Wolfe. *Thomas Wolfe and His Family*. New York: Doubleday, 1961.

Williams, William Carlos. *Paterson*. Edited by Christopher MacGowan. New York: New Directions, 1992.

Wordsworth, William. *William Wordsworth*. Edited by Stephen Gill. The Oxford Authors Series. Oxford: Oxford University Press, 1984.

Index

Abrams, M. H., 98, 100, 134n. 6, 137n. 14
Absalom, Absalom! (Faulkner), 110–11
Adams, Agatha Boyd, 38
aerial "shots," 67–68, 73. *See also* devices, Wolfe's
allusion, 45, 50
America: attitude of Wolfe toward, 6, 8, 16–17, 20–22, 26, 33–35, 42–45, 54–55, 60, 122n. 1, 123n. 11; imagery, 16, 21, 34–36, 43–44, 65, 67–68, 73–74, 112; materialism in, 3
American literature: epiphanic moments in, 120n. 9; and nature, 12–13, 16, 53, 69, 104–7; and New York City, 18–19; and romanticism, 1, 110–11; in the 1920s and 1930s, 2, 6, 15–20, 103–17. *See also* modernism
analogy, 50
Anderson, Sherwood, 7. *See also* American literature
Antaeus, or A Memory of Earth, 57, 100
Appalachia, 31
Armstrong, Anne, 54, 60
Asheville, N.C., 23, 37–38, 40–41, 129n. 6, 130n. 17
Asheville Citizen, The, 32
Asheville Daily News, 54
Asheville Times, 131n. 17

Aswell, Edward, 125n. 12, 133n. 8
autobiographical approach, 4, 6

Barnes, John S., 9
Basso, Hamilton, 35
Bate, Jonathan, 100, 136n. 3
Beach, Joseph Warren, 9–10
"Bear, The" (Faulkner), 92
Beja, Morris, 120n. 9
Benson, Jackson J., 138n. 18
Bentz, Joseph, 7
Bernstein, Aline, 3, 40, 60
"Big Two-Hearted River" (Hemingway), 16, 106
Boyle, Thomas E., 53
Bredahl, A. Carl Jr., 53
Brooklyn Bridge, 26
Brown, Kenneth, 4–5, 119n. 4
Buell, Lawrence, 10–11

Cather, Willa, 106–8, 137n. 15. *See also* American literature
character formation. *See* persona
characterizations: Cather's, 106; Faulkner's, 111; Hemingway's, 106; Wolfe's, 4, 5, 22, 28–32, 36, 49, 78, 81–88, 93, 100, 116–17, 129n. 9, 130n. 13
Charles River, 71–72. *See also* rivers
childhood: and persona, 30–32, 133n. 2; Wolfe's, 23, 32, 35, 37–41, 82

"Frigate Pelican, The" (Moore), 115
From Death to Morning, 40, 43, 44,
    45, 48, 72
Frost, Robert, 112–13. *See also*
    American literature

Gelfant, Blanche, 69, 122n. 11,
    132n. 6
Glotfelty, Cheryll, 1, 11
Goldsmith, Arnold, 69, 77
Grapes of Wrath, The (Steinbeck),
    108–9, 138n. 19
Great Depression, 59
Great Gatsby, The (Fitzgerald), 16
Green Hills of Africa (Hemingway),
    105
"green" world. *See* nature
"Gulliver," 45

Hagan, John, 135n. 1
Hay, John, 12
H. D. *See* Doolittle, Hilda (H. D.)
height, Thomas Wolfe's, 34–36,
    132n. 7
Hemingway, Ernest, 16,
    137n. 15; as compared to
    Wolfe, 104–6. *See also*
    American literature
Hills Beyond, The, 32–33, 40, 55,
    103, 134n. 6
Hinze, Diana Orendi, 120n. 8
"His Father's Earth," 33
Hoagland, Kathleen, 44
Holliday, Shawn, 123n. 6
Holman, Hugh, 123n. 6, 125n. 12,
    135n. 11

Hound of Darkness, The, 68, 79,
    128n. 3, 132n. 2
Hudson River, 74, 75
Huntley, Reid, 135n. 2

Idaho, 34, 36
Idol, John L. Jr., 3, 119n. 5, 120n. 6,
    134n. 6
imagery: America, 16, 34, 35–36,
    65, 67–68, 73–74; animal,
    46–47, 78; hills, 40–41;
    "imported" landscape, 75–77, 80;
    natural: —, *Look Homeward,
    Angel*, 37–38, 39, 40, 41, 48,
    59, 63–65, 70, 79, 81–94, 97,
    99, 102, 105–6, 108, 123n. 6,
    126n. 14, 135n. 7; —, *Of Time
    and the River*, 12, 39, 40–42,
    58–59, 63, 66–68, 70, 71, 73,
    74–75, 76, 79, 114, 123n. 8,
    126n. 14; —, *The Web and the
    Rock*, 40, 42, 44–45, 46, 47, 52,
    65–66, 69–71, 73–75, 79, 99,
    103, 117; Wolfe's use of, 1–2,
    8–10, 11–12, 13–15, 18, 20–27,
    33–34, 37–38, 61, 132n. 1; *You
    Can't Go Home Again*, 40–41,
    47–48, 52, 57–58, 59, 71, 79–80,
    102; sea, 39, 44–45, 91, 95,
    128n. 3, 129n. 7; seasonal, 20,
    57, 61–62, 86, 91, 92, 94, 96,
    111; sensual, 88–89; urban,
    18–20, 30, 69, 73–75,
    124n. 10, 126n. 13, 132n. 6
immortality, earthly, 40–42,
    45, 56–57, 59, 74, 91, 94, 128n. 3

"imported" landscape imagery, 75–77, 80. *See also* devices, Wolfe's

In Our Time (Hemingway), 16, 105

"In the Park," 72

Jeffers, Robinson, 116

Johnston, Carol Ingalls, 120n. 6

joy, 100–101. *See also* emotion

Joyce, James, 7, 17, 64

Kennedy, Richard, 5, 123n. 4

Kowalewski, Michael, 10

Kroeber, Karl, 4, 97, 100–101, 136n. 3

Kussy, Bella, 123n. 5

language, use of, 53, 69, 112, 115; and criticism, 10–11, 110; Hemingway's, 105; —, in *Look Homeward, Angel*, 24; —, in *The Web and the Rock*, 24; Wolfe's, 8, 12, 15, 16–17, 61, 72, 77, 97; —, in *You Can't Go Home Again*, 55–56

Lee, Russel V., 60

Lemmon, Elizabeth, 54, 124n. 8

Lewis, Sinclair, 3

"Life from the Lifeless" (Jeffers), 116

London, 20, 27, 43

Look Homeward, Angel, 3, 5, 39, 41, 80, 116, 129n. 7, 133n. 2; American imagery in, 43–44; animal imagery in, 46, 47, 78; effect of place on persona in, 31; environmental connectedness in, 28, 29, 45, 50, 56, 80, 81–96; Joycean

influences in, 7; language in, 24; natural imagery in, 37–38, 39, 40, 41, 48, 59, 63–65, 70, 79, 81–94, 97, 99, 102, 105–6, 108, 123n. 6, 126n. 14, 135n. 7; seasonal context in, 61–62; subjective point of view, 22

Love, Glen, 13, 137n. 15

lyricism, 4, 8–10. *See also* language, use of

Machor, James L., 53

Magi, Aldo, 44, 55, 131n. 17

Marx, Leo, 131n. 14

"Men of Old Catawba, The," 56

metaphor, 19, 63, 69, 77, 79–80, 94, 137n. 14; Hemingway's use of, 16; trees as, 71, 73

mindscapes, 66–67

"Minor Bird, A" (Frost), 113

Mississippi River, 32, 39, 44, 90. *See also* rivers

modernism, 2, 68–69; devices of, 7, 15–16, 82, 110–11; and *Look Homeward, Angel*, 82–83, 133n. 3; themes of, 7; and truth in writing, 15–17, 41, 105; and Wolfe, 6–8, 14, 116. *See also* American literature; romanticism

moonlight ("moonscapes"), 66, 70, 132n. 4, 135n. 7. *See also* imagery

Moore, Marianne, 115–16. *See also* American literature

mountains, 29, 40, 41, 60, 67, 84–85, 90–91, 93, 101, 127n. 2, 128n. 4, 134n. 6

Wordsworth, William, 82, 98–100,
102, 131n. 15, 133n. 2, 136n. 5,
137n. 10
World War I, 15

You Can't Go Home Again: aerial
"shot" in, 67; America
imagery in, 21, 34, 35–36;
animal imagery in, 46, 78;
city imagery in, 74–76; effect
of place on persona in, 30; emotion and landscape, 134n. 5;
environmental connectedness in,
50, 54; language in, 55–56; natural imagery in, 40–41, 47–48, 52,
57–58, 59, 71, 79–80, 102;
personification in, 101;
vitalism in, 18